Hindu Festivals in Mauritius

Chand S Seewoochurn

Editions Capucines

© Chand S Seewoochurn, 1995

ISBN 99903-916-0-2

Set by Chand S. Seewoochurn
Quatre Bornes, Mauritius

Printed at the Mauritius Printing Specialists (Pte) ltd
Stanley, Mauritius

Editions Capucines
Quatre Bornes, Mauritius
Tel/Fax (230) 464 1563

My Mothers

Hardevi and Mekhul Sootha

Cover Design   Moorthi Nagalingum

Photographs

Courtesy   Ougesh Bundhun
               Aneerood Jugroop
               Bhaskar Rughoonundon

               Hari Har Chetra Mandir, Quatre Bornes
               Brindaban Sarva Janik Mandir, Palma
               Tulsi Shyam Mandir, Beau Bassin
               Mauritiuseswar Nath Shiv Jyotir Lingam Mandir, Grand Bassin

Contents

Preface	
Introduction	11
Makara Sankranti	19
Vasant Panchami	23
Maha Shivaratri	26
Lakshmi Ashtami	31
Holi	33
Nav Varsh	37
Rama Navmi	40
Hanuman Jayanti	46
Jankee Jayanti	50
Parvati Jayanti	52
Ganga Dussehra	56
Gayatri Jayanti	58
Nirjala Ekadashi	60
Vata Savitri Vrat	62
Kabir Jayanti	64
Guru Purnima	67
Naag Panchami	69
Tulsidas Jayanti	72
Raksha Bandhan	77
Krishna Janmasthami	80
Hartalika Vrat	86
Ganesh Chaturti	88
Rishi Panchami	93
Maha Ravivar Vrat	95
Radha Ashtami	99
Anant Chaturdashi	102

Pitra Paksh	105
Jivit Putrika Vrat	107
Durga Navmi	110
Vijay Dashmi	118
Karak Chaturthi Vrat	119
Dhana Teras	122
Narak Chaturdashi Yam	125
Divali	128
Govardhan Puja	132
Yam Dwitiya Bhaiya Duja	133
Surya Chát Vrat	135
Prabhodhini Ekadashi	137
Vaikunth Chaturdashi	140
Ganga Snan	141
Guru Nanak	145
Shri Sathya Sai Baba	147
Gita Jayanti	152
Bibliography	156
Glossary	157

Author's Note

Hindu Festivals in Mauritius is the first volume in the series *Festivals in Mauritius* which aims at providing the whole community of the island researched information about the festivals observed in Mauritius, thus bringing about a sharing of knowledge, understanding and meaning. As one would note there is a continuous flow of festivals throughout the year - some being well known and widely celebrated, and others being less known and confined to small groups. Of late an awakening of religious fervour throughout the island has been observed, in particular among the youths, who clamour for deeper knowledge of and fuller participation in the festivals. Hence the need to bring out this series of *Festivals in Mauritius,* which through all its volumes, hopes to be able to do justice to most of the festivals celebrated by the different groups.

The festivals dealt with in *Hindu Festivals in Mauritius* are those listed in the *Calendar of Fasts and Festivals* by the main socio-cultural organisations. They are mainly observed by people of Hindu origin coming from the northern part of India. The number and variety are amazing, some being very popular and others of lesser appeal. Festivals like *Durga Navmi* which were once held within the precincts of a few traditional households have found expression in wider circles today, and others as the *Karwa Chaut* and *Yam Dwitiya Bhaiya Duja,* which till recently were almost unheard of have made an appearance. This work has been inspired by notes (from a tattered notebook) compiled by late Pandit Bhimsen Bajpai, and through information and knowledge imparted to me through a *guru-shisya* schooling, by his brother Indrasen, son Kavi, and nephew Pyare Bajpai. The other sources of information have been from publications listed in the bibliography.

The project has called for help and assistance from a large group of people. Most of them have been alive and quick in their response to my appeal. I am pleasantly surprised to recall how we were all kept together, bound in affection and esteem, during the course of this work. I am most grateful to all, but to do justice to all here would be an impossible task. However I would like to mention a few among whom Sir Dayendranath Burrenchobay whose spontaneous expression of delight has encouraged me to see the project through.

Other persons who deserve special mention are my former colleagues at the Mahatma Gandhi Institute, in particular Moorthi, Shameela, Jeewon, Ibrahim, and Dev, and all my other former colleagues of the Mauritius Printing Specialists (Pte) Ltd. My niece Sheila, cousin Aswini, brother-in-law Suren, and friend Robin have throughout this work been my treasured companions. And finally the members of my own family - Divya, Michael and Indira, have provided me with all the support that such a task entails. My thanks and deep gratitude are here expressed to all.

Preface

The Hindus came to Mauritius in successive waves of immigration from diverse regions of India from 1835 to around 1920. Most of them came from the north-eastern bhojpuri-speaking provinces of Bihar. Many came from the South of India, from the Tamil-speaking and the Telegu-speaking provinces of Madras and Andhra Pradesh. And yet a few came from the Marathi-speaking regions of Bombay and from Gujrat.

If in their baggage they had brought few material belongings, in the depths of their being they had brought with them a millenary culture going back to Vedic and pre-vedic times. They were deeply religious and lost no time in installing their gods and goddesses in their homes, in the village shrines and temples. Finding themselves in a hostile and alien environment they clung resolutely to their customs and traditions and it is amazing how, despite the inhuman living conditions that prevailed at the time and despite repeated attempts to deculturise them, they managed to preserve their distinct values, beliefs and traditions.

India, their country of origin, is a vast country of infinite variety and diversity. It is a land inhabited by millions of people of different races, speaking over 150 languages and dialects. There are festivals common to all Indians, and there are others characteristic of particular regions.

Mauritius had inherited the religious unity and also the cultural heterogeneity of the Indian sub-continent. But on this little acre, the Hindus from the North, from the South and West were brought closer culturally. But like in India, there are festivals common to all Hindus and there are others which are characteristic of particular linguistic groups.

Hindu Festivals in Mauritius, the first of a new series, focuses on the festivals celebrated principally by the bhojpuri-speaking Hindus, originating from the north-eastern province of Bihar, which represent the majority Hindu group. Some of these festivals are equally observed by all Hindus, irrespective of their places of origin.

We are now in the process of rapid economic and cultural transformation. The processes set in motion by historical and international factors favour the dissemination of Western norms and values. The Hindus of Mauritius now stand at the crossroads of their cultural destiny.

The present generation is still as deeply attached to their ancient traditions as ever, although they have also incorporated modern norms and values. We have a duty to impart to the youths of today and to future generations as much information as possible about the customs and traditions, rites and rituals, celebrations and other observances which constitute their heritage.

This book will no doubt help in this task while at the same time it will help generate informed interest in one of the greatest cultural and religious traditions of mankind.

Ramesh Ramdoyal

Introduction

Festivals are held in communities, and communities draw inspiration from religion which is a set of established rules based on ethics and moral conduct. In course of time the rules, as a result of social, economic and political development, do undergo changes. However the innate concept of moral values and philosophy always predominates because it embodies the everlasting sterling qualities of goodness, truth and righteousness. And festivals being part and parcel of that truth keep on pulsating with life however remote their birth could be.

Hindu Religion

Hindu Religion, like any other religion, has the underlying concept of goodness, truth, and righteousness summarised as *dharma*. This *dharma* embodies the main teachings of the *Vedas* regarding conduct, discipline in life, philosophy and rituals, and as such is commonly referred to as the *Aryan religion* or *Arya Dharma* or *Sanatana Dharma* (perennial religion). *Dharma* is imperishable. It is indispensable not only to the world of matter, but also a *sine qua non* to the life of emotion, intellect and consciousness of each and every individual. And to the society, as every individual has to move and interact with one another in a group according to the perennial laws of nature.

Dharma has withstood the test of time. It is about 5,000 years old, and seemingly the oldest. In spite of its moments of despair and decay through the many invasions and incursions, it has always managed to keep awakening again and again and breathing with life through the appearance of seers and saints. The *dharma*, as practised by the Hindus is also known as Hinduism. However to confine Hinduism to *dharma* only is to deny justice to it. Hinduism is an all embracing word, and defining it would be a collossal, nay an impossible task.

The Aryans and the Vedas

The word Hindu originates from the name *Sindhu*, the greatest river of India. Hindu means people, and most probably refers to the Aryans who might have migrated from the southern steppes of Russia possibly between the period 1700 and 700 B.C to settle on the banks of that river. They came to India with their sacred texts, the *Vedas*. Their language, the Sanskrit, is related to some European languages such as Greek and Latin, as also some of their gods. The Sanskrit word *Veda* derives from *vid* (to know) and literally means science - and science itself deriving from the Latin word *scire* (to know). The Vedic age has been one of great intellect, scientific consciousness and mystic disciplines. The *Vedas* are replete with spiritual and philosophical composition. The *Vedas* are -

(1) *Rig Veda* containing hymns in praise of the divine being.

(2) *Yajur Veda* dealing with religious rites and sacrifices.

(3) *Soma Veda* containing hymns of peace and praise to the living intelligences and powers in nature.

Rishi Atharva created another *Veda*, the *Atharva Veda* by taking the quintessence of the above three *Vedas*. The *Atharva Veda* deals with the duties and responsibilities of mankind.

The *Vedas* are the only scriptures of the Aryans available today, the other scriptures having been washed away by the tide of time or digested in the cruelty of invasion.

In addition to the *Vedas* other authorities in Indian literature are the *Epics* and the *Upanishads*. The two great epics are the *Ramayana* and the *Mahabharata* written between 300 BC and AD 300. The *Ramayana* tells the story of Rama who came to the earth to relieve her of the burden of the demon king Ravana, and to shed light on the model behaviour of man. The *Mahabharata* is woven with the story of the cousins, *Pandavas* and *Kauravas,* and their conflict. The quintessence is the great *Bhagavad Gita*, the discourse given by Krishna to Arjuna on the battlefield of Kurukshetra.

The *Upanishads* are the main interpretations of the *Vedas*, giving their essence. There are 118 *Upanishads*, but 12 of them are considered to be the most important and popular. They are *Isa, Kena, Katha, Prasna, Mundaka, Markandeya, Aitareya, Taittiriya, Chhandogya, Brihadaranyaka, Kaushitcha* and *Svetasvatara*. One meaning of the word *Upanishad* is 'sitting near', as pupil and teacher. Another meaning is 'secret doctrine'. However both meanings fit in as the teachings were passed on orally in a *guru-shishya* (teacher-disciple) relationship and given in a very austere and pure spirit.

Brahman

Both the *Vedas*, in particular the *Rig Veda,* and the *Puranas* mention of prayers to the gods, and are replete with narrations of wars between the *devas* (gods) and the *asuras* (demons). The *devas* (gods) are the illumined ones and represent light for knowledge and wisdom, while the *asuras* (demons) are the forces of darkness and ignorance. And in any struggle between these forces the victory of the divinity is assured. The victory of Rama over Ravana, that of Krishna over Kansa, and the defeat of Mahishasura by divine Mother Durga indeniably support this view. This shining principle, the truth, is common to all deities. In the *Upanishads* it is revealed as *Brahman*. It is the '*One*' and at the same time the '*Many*'. '*One*' is the essence and '*Many*' are its manifestations. This is advocated again and again, by all sects, cults and doctrines in the Hindu religion as was already stated in the *Rig Veda* (1.164.46) '*Ekam sat vipra bahudha vedanti*' - *Truth is one, sages call It by various names.*' And the goal of human life is the realisation of this *Brahman*, the attainment of *moksha* (liberation) which means releasing oneself from the cycle of birth and death (*samsara*).

Hindus are therefore monotheists. Although praying different gods - Vishnu, Shiva, Durga - the ultimate godhead to whom the worship is addressed is *Brahman*. Monotheism and pantheism are not contradictory but complimentary to each other. The Vedic seers identified their Supreme Being with Infinity which pervaded and contained all the countless universes with their earths, oceans, skies, solar systems and the planets. All the processes of creation, maintenence and destruction in the Universe were sustained within that Infinity. Nothing remained outside Him -

"That God is full. This - the manifestation - is full. From that this has come. Even after this has come out of that that remains full"

Om purnamadah purnamidam purnamudachyate purnasya purnamadaya purnamevaava-sishyate.

Deities

The Aryans laid emphasis on the fundamental and abstract conceptions and natural phenomena such as the *Surya* (Sun), *Vayu* (Wind), *Agni* (Fire), *Chandrama* (Moon). The *Vedas* contain rather detailed descriptions of the ceremonies practised to coerce the deities to grant material benefits to the worshipper. These deities, it seems, were sometimes visualised as having human or animal form, but it should not be concluded that they were worshipped in the form of images. There is however, the possibility that some of the lower strata, the indigeneous population used to worship images in human and animal form, and the practices could have spread across and upward in the communities, and in course of time the Vedic deities were retrospectively given human and animal form and reproduced as images.

Following the Aryans' further penetration and their intimacy with the indigenous population, supported by the inevitable forces of development some of the concepts in the deities should have undergone changes. Some of the deities changed their functions, gained or lost their prestige. Eventually the gods who were confirmed for worship were the result of the fusion of ideas brought by the invading Aryans and the indigenous inhabitants. The Brahmins could have been instrumental to some extent in bringing about a change in the concept. The powers of intercession between the deity and the layman were confined to them and they enjoyed the monopoly for performing sacrifices. The Vedic deities as *Agni* (Fire), *Vayu* (Wind), *Surya* (Sun), *Soma* (Moon), and *Indra* (God of Rain) could have been moved to minor positions in the pantheon at the expense of other deities, and the introduction of new deities could well have taken place.

The *Ramayana* and the *Mahabharata*, the two great epics, have stimulated further more personal relationship between gods and men. The stories not only describe the feats of the heroic characters but refer to the influence that the gods had on their exploits. And the heroic characters being beautifully expanded and majestically woven in the stories became so popular that they gradually got assimilated in the mind as deities.

The further development of the Indian society brought about changes in various planes, and consequently corresponding religious concepts underwent some change. The size of the pantheon increased. The minor Vedic deity Vishnu was moved to the highest place of prominence. Simultaneously ancient fertility god, Shiva was promoted to an equally dignified position. Finally together with Vishnu and Shiva, Brahma whose name had hardly appeared in the *Vedas* was incorporated to form the triad - Brahma, Vishnu and Shiva. However Brahma never became so popular but the widespread adoration of Vishnu and Shiva continued producing, the two sects *Vaishnavs* and *Shaivites*. Thus the Vedic earlier most prominent triad -*Agni* (Fire), *Vayu* (Wind) and *Surya* (Sun) was moved to a lower position.

Together with the establishment of the Brahmanical triad - Brahma, Vishnu and Shiva, the worship of female deities was promoted. Saraswati, Lakshmi and Parvati the consorts of the triad gods became their *shaktis*. This idea was not new as the concept of creative power did exist in the Vedic time. The *Rig Veda* in trying to elucidate the mystery of creation mentions that the Creator willed to create the Universe through the agency of a female principle. The idea was expressed in the supposed marriage of heaven and earth. Mention is also made of the existence of the *linga* and the *yoni* which were locked up as a representation of creative power. The Supreme Goddess, was linked to Rudra, from whom Shiva seems to have originated, as his *shakti* (power). Shiva is the *linga* (phallic emblem) and Parvati the *yoni* (female emblem). The development of Tantrism, further emphasized the cult of the female partner (*shakti*) in association with her consort. The combined representation of Lord Shiva and Mother Goddess Parvati as *Ardhanavishwar* (half of god and half of shakti) is well known. The concept of *Brahman* and *Shakti* is indentical. Energy in its static condition is *Brahman*, and with its evolving aspect is *Shakti*.

Lately in the 1960s the cult of Santoshi Mata with her own mythology and legends has come up. And very recently the birth of Sai Baba has crept in as an *avatar*.

Image worship

Image worship is the worship of the Eternal Reality through symbols - attempting to reach the Infinite through limited vision, the spiritual through the material, the invisible through the visible, the universal through the individual, and the timeless, spaceless and formless whole through fragments. The Hindu philosophical teachings inspire the devotee with the idea that God is omnipresent, omniscient and omnipotent. He dwells in all objects animate and inanimate. Hence all represent God to him. The mother, the father and the *guru* are gods and in visible forms. This concept is extended to the idols and images which soon breathe with life. Their sight generates an exciting feeling of adoration. As the days go by, the faith in the idol deepens, and at each step the devotee feels nearer to him. He gets close to him, he speaks to him in his language, and trusts him. To make it easier to concentrate, sometimes the theory of *Ishta Devata* (chosen deity) is applied. The worshipper is required to concentrate on the deity congenial to his nature with the help of a *mantra*.

The spiritual training through the daily prayer and adoration tunes up the mind of the devotee who is set on the path of perfection and purity. He is inspired to seek self-realisation. When wisdom dawns upon him he becomes aware that this idol worship is but a stepping stone to the Higher Truth. Thus idol worship is not the end in itself. It serves the purpose of realising Supreme Godhead, otherwise difficult, even impossible for many spiritual aspirants.

Performing the Puja

The idol is considered as an honoured guest. He is a visitor and may be tired reaching the host's residence after his long and tedious journey. Everything is done to relieve him of his fatigue, and all arrangements are made so that his visit becomes pleasant. He is given a seat, followed by water for his personal cleaning and drinking. He is offered clothing and ornaments. Flowers, fruits and sweets are given. All is done to the tune of music - ringing of bells, beating of drums and blowing of conches. Prayers are chanted in his honour. When the worship is completed and the guest is ready to leave, he is sent away with all ceremony.

Worship should be done with faith, devotion and reverence. The devotee has first and foremost to purify himself both physically and spiritually. He must have his mind tuned so that the *puja* is carried out successfully and with lasting effect. Initially the *avahan* (invocation) is done when the god or goddess is invited to take abode in the idol or image. The rituals can be done in five steps, known as the *Pancho Pachar Pujanam* or in sixteen steps called the *Sohraso Pachar Pujanam*. The *Labdho Pachar Pujanam* is another way of performing rituals where mostly articles at hand are offered.

The *Pancho Pachar Pujanam* can be carried out through -

1. *Padyam* - Offering water for washing the feet.
2. *Arghyam* - Offering water as done while giving *arag*.
3. *Dupam* – Burning incense (sandal stick).
4. *Dipam* - Waving of light
5. *Naivadyam* - Offering of food.

The *Sohraso Pachar Pujanam* involves the undermentioned but are subject to variation. For example the need for the first two steps does not arise if the *puja* is being performed to an already consecrated idol such as those in a *shivala*.

1. *Avahanam* - Inviting the god/goddess to take abode in the image.
2. *Asanam* - Offering a seat to the god/goddess.
3. *Padyam* - Offering water for washing the feet.
4. *Argyam* - Offering water as done while giving *arag*.
5. *Atchmanyam* - Offering water for rinsing the mouth.
6. *Snanam* - Offering water for ablution.
7. *Vastram, Yagyo Pavitram* - Offering raiment, and *janeo* to male deities
8. *Chandanam/Gandham* - Applying sandal paste.
9. *Abiram, Kumkumam, Sinduram, Akshatam* - Applying *Puspam* coloured powder, rice and offering flowers.
10. *Dhupam* - Burning incense.
11. *Dipam* - Waving of light.
12. *Naivaidyam* - Offering food.
13. *Achmanyam* - Offering water for rinsing of mouth.

14. *Tambulam and Poungipalam* - Offering nuts and betel leaves.
15. *Dakshinam* - Giving presents - usually gift in coins
16. *Pushpanjali* - Offering flowers with both hands.

When the above rituals are completed prayers are chanted in his honour. The idol is worshipped through *mantras* and *prayers* and recitations from sacred texts. The *pradakshina* (circumambulation) is done, and blessings are requested from the god or goddess for either material or spiritual progress or both. Devotees apologise for any shortcoming in the *puja* through *mantras*. One of the fitting *mantras* is -

*"Avahanamm na janami, najanami visharjanam
Puja chaiva na janami, chamiataam parmeswarah."*

And finally the *puja* is closed by doing the *visarjan* through which the god or goddess is sent back with all due honour. One would note that while performing any *puja* the first prayers are usually addressed to Lord Ganesha.

Most Hindu festivals involve rituals and the above may serve as a common denominator for their performance with the exception of a few. However given the size of the pantheon and the specific attributes of some of the deities, the need would undoubtedly arise for variance and adjuncts. The help and participation of a *guru* or an officiating priest is a *sine qua non,* and the above should in no case be considered as a substitute for his absence. It should rather trigger imagination, and arouse a quest for wider knowledge which would drive towards fuller participation in the *puja*.

Makara Sankranti

Sankranti comes from the word *sankraman* which means the passing of the Sun from one *rasi* (Zodiac sign) to the next. Since we have twelve *rasis* we therefore have twelve *Sankrantis* in a year. These *rasis* are *Mesh* (Aries), *Vrishabha* (Taurus), *Mithuna* (Gemini), *Karka* (Cancer), *Simha* (Leo), *Kanya* (Virgin), *Tula* (Libra), *Vrischika* (Scorpio), *Dhanus* (Sagittarius), *Makara* (Capricorn), *Kumbha* (Aquarius), *Meena* (Pisces).

Makara Sankranti is considered as the most important of all the *Sankrantis*. It is on the first day of the *Makara rasi*. The festival is usually held on the fourteenth of January. However in some circumstances it can take place a day before or a day after, taking into consideration the most auspicious time for its observance.

Day and Night

It is believed that a year is divided into two parts, day and night, for the gods. The six month period from mid-January to mid-July constitutes the day, and the period mid-July to mid-January the night. Alternatively the year consisting of twelve *rasis,* six *rasis* beginning from the *Makara rasi* account for the day and the other six *rasis* starting from the *Karka rasi* constitute the night.

As *Makara Sankranti* sanctions the dawn of the day for the gods they start by worshipping their Supreme Being, the Sun-God. Taking to this belief devotees too perform rituals for the Sun, but at the same time pray and invoke the blessings of other gods. The Sun is considered as one of the most powerful deities. It provides light and warmth, and its influence in the economy is beyond doubt the source of all success. Some names of the Sun-God are Diwakara (*Day Maker*), Bhaskara (*Giver of Light*) Prabhakara (*Bestower of Light*) and Grahapat (*King of the Planets*).

Devotees offer prayers to Lord Vishnu too on the occasion of this festival. The day is considered very auspicious for holding *pujas* like the *Satyanarain Swami ki Katha* in honour of Lord Vishnu, or celebrating the *Dhaja puja* for Lord Hanuman. If a *Sankranti* falls on a Sunday and is the seventh day of the bright fortnight of a month it is called a *Maha Jaya Sankranti*. The day is most favourable for divine communion. In Vedic times the Sun with the other two gods Wind and Fire formed the gods of the Trimurti, *Agni - Vayu - Surya* (Fire-Wind-Sun).

Celebrating Sankranti

In Mauritius the house, in particular the *puja ghar* (prayer room) is thoroughly cleaned on the eve. The festival is celebrated by waking up early, taking a bath and worshipping the deities, in particular the Sun as stated earlier. Devotees offer flowers, fruits, *prasad* (cereals cooked in milk) or *ladoo* (sweet balls) made of flour, sugar and *til* (sesame seeds). The ceremony outside the house usually consists of lighting a new earthen lamp at the *chawtra* (shrine), offering flowers and prayers, and giving the *arag* to the Sun in the east. The *arag* involves standing reverentially and pouring water gently from a *lota* (pot) to the ground, accompanied by *mantras*.

After the rituals the members of the family greet one another. Younger ones salute the elders as a token of regard to seek their blessings. Children are donned with new clothes and receive gifts, which consist mostly of notes and coins. *Sankranti* is not

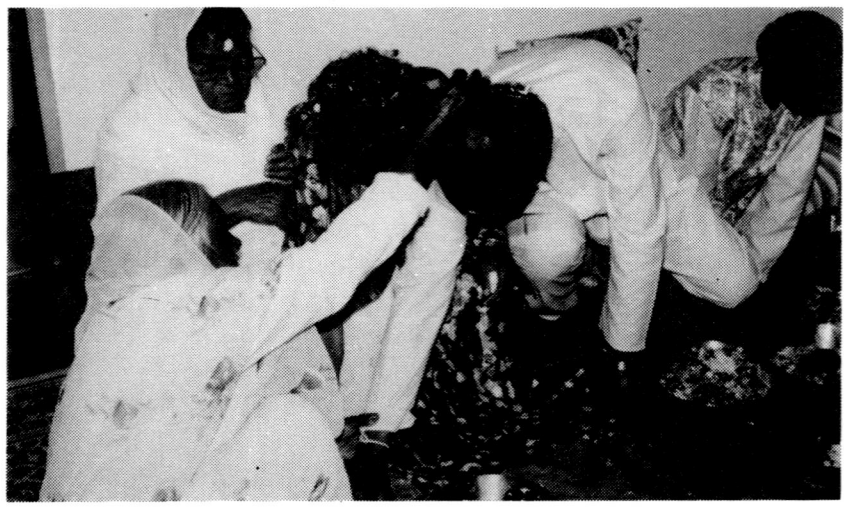

Seeking blessings from elders

the austere festival which is usually accompanied by fasting and penance. A special menu for the occasion is the *kitchri*. It is made of rice and dholl cooked together, with different spices added. Saffron is one of the cherished ingredients as it symbolises freshness and prosperity. The side dish consists of tomato *chutney* and fried potatoes. Devotees spend the afternoon by paying visits to relatives and friends, or by being just on their own. It is a day when devotees offer *daan* (gifts) to their *gurus*. Charitable institutions are visited with a view to relieving the miseries of the needy. The festival may possibly be of agrarian origin taking into consideration that on this day in some parts of India meals are prepared with the first grain harvested, but with the passage of time it may have been imbued with religious content of meaning. Historically, January being the coldest month, people might have prayed for the cold snap of the month with its sultry and gloomy sky to give way to the warmth and radiant sunshine of the summer months.

It was a practice for some devotees and still is in many traditional households in Mauritius to perform the *puja* in a more elaborate way. They make a dough with flour and spread it flat on the ground. Others may simply spread white flour on a large steel plate. They design twelve 'houses' at the edge at equal distances to represent the twelve *rasis*. In the centre they draw the picture of the Sun to convey the meaning that the *rasis* are subject to its influence. Those good at art use coloured powder to decorate the plate and the 'houses'.

Rituals are performed through the *pancho pachar* or *sohraso pachar pujanam*. This involves invoking and welcoming the deities, offering flowers, coloured powder *(abir, kumkum* and *sindour)*, *akshat* (rice) and sundry fruits, and waving light. The main offerings, as stated earlier, are *prasad* and *ladoo*. Prayers are chanted to all deities, and to the Sun using red flowers. The Sun is meditated upon with one of these *mantras* "Om Bhaskaraya Namaha, "Om Dinkaraya Namaha", "Om Prabhakaraya Namaha", "Om Suryaye Namaha", or "Om Diwakaraye Namaha", repeated 108 times using the *jap mala* (rosary). A fitting prayer for the Sun God is -

" *Aadi deva namastubhyam prasseeda mama bhaskara Divaakara namastubhyam prabhaakara namostute.*"

The Festival in India

The festival is celebrated in almost all parts of India though with slightly varying attributes. Big fairs are held in holy cities like Hardwar and Vrindavan and ritual bath is taken in the sacred rivers of Ganga, Jamuna, and Saraswati to purify onself. Since the festival takes place in the month of *Magha* (January/February) it is also known as the *Magha Mela*. In some regions of India, the festival is dedicated to prayers for a rich harvest. In the coastal regions it is held in honour of Indra, Lord of Rain.

In South India, it is a harvest festival known as *Pongal Sankranti* and is celebrated for three days. The first day, *Bhogi Pongal,* is celebrated among members of the family. They light a bonfire and burn useless articles and clothes in it. They sing and dance round the bonfire just as is done for the *Lohri* festival which is celebrated about the same time by the Punjab community. The second day is the *Surya Pongal* and the Sun-God is worshipped with rice boiled in milk and jaggery. *Pongal* in fact means 'boiled' and when friends and relatives meet they ask: "Has it boiled?" The reply would be -"Yes, it has". It is a day of great joy and rejoicing. The third day, *Mattu Pongal*, is dedicated to honouring the cattle (*mattu)* by cleaning, feeding, garlanding and imbuing them with love.

In Mauritius devotees of South Indian origin celebrate *Sankranti* on the *Surya Pongal* day. Devotees make a hearth outside in the yard, and have rice, milk and sugar boiled in an earthen pot (*panai*). When the dish is ready, they perform the rituals facing the Sun. They spread a plantain leaf on which they lay the *pongal* and other offerings. They offer prayers to the Sun and break their fast with the *prasad* (offerings).

In West Bengal devotees go on pilgrimage in particular to the river Ganga. They have a bath to purify themselves and pay homage to Mother Ganga. They take the holy water of the river to be sprinkled in the house on auspicious days. At the time of death the sacred water mixed with *tulsi* (basil) leaf is given to the departing soul to relieve him of his mundane pain and miseries, to purify him and to pave the way for a safe journey into the next world. In Mauritius this water, if not available, water from the *Ganga Talao* considered as the *Ganga Jal,* is widely used to the same end.

Mother Saraswati

Vasant Panchami

Vasant Panchami is held on the *panchami* (fifth day) of the bright half *(suklapaksh)* of *Magha* (January/February). It is dedicated to Mother Saraswati, Goddess of Speech, Learning and Fine Arts. Other gods as Ganesha, Vishnu, Shiva and Surya are also worshipped on this day. This festival is also called the *Shishir Panchami* as it is held in the *shishir* season which is between winter and spring in India. In some parts of India it is known as *Magh Sukla Panchami*.

In India *Vasant Panchami* heralds spring *(vasant)* with all its sweetness and mirth. Many of the trees are in blossom in the fields, in particular, the *sarson* (mustard) which gives a tinge of yellow. Yellow is the symbol of warmth and auspiciousness. This colour is projected in as many ways as possible. Devotees wear new clothes in yellow, prepare food and tinge it yellow with saffron, and perform rituals using yellow flowers.

वसन्त पंचमी

श्री शारदां प्रार्थित सिद्ध विधां ।
श्री शारदाम्भोज संगोत्र नेत्राम् ॥
श्री शारदाम्भोज निवीज्यमानां ।
श्री शारदाङ्क कानुजनि भजामि ॥

Shree shaaradaam praarthita siddha vidyaam
Shree shaaradaambhoja sagotra netraam
Shree shaaradaambhoja niveejya maanaam
Shree shaaradaankaanujanim

Saraswati

Saraswati is the spouse of Brahma. According to a legend it is believed that Lord Vishnu had three wives - Parvati, Saraswati and Lakshmi. He found it hard to cope with three wives and, therefore, gave Parvati to Lord Shiva, Saraswati to Lord Brahma and kept Lakshmi for Himself. Such a story may not hold good. However we may have to consider another legend where it is said that only Lord Maha Vishnu and His wife existed in the beginningless time before the creation of the universe. He then had to split Himself into three different bodies with specific attributes for each of them - Brahma as Creator, Vishnu as Preserver and Shiva as Destroyer. As such a partner had to be found for each. Hence the creation by Maha Vishnu of the most righteous and sweet-tempered Saraswati for Brahma, the beautiful Lakshmi for Vishnu and the compassionate Parvati for Shiva. Creation should not conjure the meaning of giving birth to an offspring as it is commonly understood by the human intellect today. Creation could take place through *manshik shristi* (mind-

born - creation by the mind) unlike *methunik shristi* where the reproductive organs had their role to fulfill.

Goddess of Speech, Learning and Arts

Speech in the very old days had a very essential role to play as all knowdedge and entire texts had to be committed to memory and passed on to the next generation by word of mouth only. This medium reached its pinnacle at the time when the *Vedas* were being brought together and imparted to succeeding generations by *gurus* to their disciples. This importance culminated in giving very high respect and reverence to the medium which soon developed into a cult of deification. In the time that followed, learning did not restrict itself to studies of scriptures only but with the development in the chain of ideas it was extended to music and the arts. The deity Saraswati most probably being the consort and active power of Brahma, Originator of the *Vedas*, was given the attributes of speech, learning and arts. Saraswati is also known as Brahmi as the consort of Brahma, and Her other names are Saradha (Giver of Essence), Vagisvari (Mistress of Speech). Saraswati also implies 'flowing in' and connected with fertility and purification. Following these attributes She is linked to the river Saraswati which flows in Rajasthan. Rivers in India and other parts of the world are revered because of their fecundity properties. They symbolise for their worshippers the concept of fertility and abundance. 'Flowing in', taken metaphorically can well relate to speech.

Goddess of Speech, Learning and Fine Arts

Saraswati is usually seen in white garments sitting on a white lotus, symbolising purity. Her favourite companions are a peacock and a swan. She has four hands. She holds the *veena* (lute) with two hands, in the third hand She has the rosary and in the last a book. At other times She may be seen with only two hands holding the lute. There may be a book, a pen and an inkstand in front of Her. However in both cases the meaning is that She is the bestower of speech, knowledge and art. And students first pay reverence to Her before embarking on their studies. Artists place their musical instruments on the altar where among all deities She holds prominence, and before performing always revere Her. The *puja* is done with welcoming rituals, offerings and recitations of prayers as done for other deities. The special offering is the *ladoo* (sweetball) made of gram flour and *til* (sesame seeds).

Kamadeva

On this memorable day Lord Shiva burnt Kamadeva, God of Love. The gods oppressed by the mighty demon, Tarakasura went to Bramha who informed them that only a son born out of the wedlock of Shiva and Parvati could kill him. As Lord Shiva was in a trance, absorbed in *samadhi,* the gods requested Kamadeva to wake Him up. Accompanied by his wife, Rati and his companion, *Vasanta* (Spring), Kamadeva called at Lord Shiva's place of *samadhi* . He shot his arrow. Lord Shiva was awakened and full of anger, burnt Kamadeva with His third eye. Rati begged for forgiveness and Lord Shiva brought him back to life. However she was told that he would not be in a visible form but would respond to the hearts of all lovers. Of Shiva`s union with Parvati, Skanda was born who killed Tarakasura.

Maha Shivaratri

A *Shivaratri puja* is performed on the *madyaratri chaturdashi* (middle of the fourteenth night) in the dark fortnight (*krishna-paksh*) of every month. The one celebrated in the month of *Phalguna* (February/March) is known as the *Maha Shivaratri* (*Maha* - Great, *Shiv* - Shiva, *ratri* - night), the Great Night of Lord Shiva. It is the main festival in honour of Lord Shiva.

Pilgrimage

The festival is preceded by days of penance. Devotees keep to a disciplined life away from sensual gratifications. They abstain from non vegetarian food and alcoholic drinks. Those going on pilgrimage even give up taking salt in food, spending the days on sweet meals only. They make their *kanwars*, structures made of bamboo stems or light *ravenal*, decorated with coloured cloth and paper, and decked with mirrors, tinkling bells and images of deities. The *kanwars* vary in size, design and colour. All shoulder one or the other on their pilgrimage.

While in India, devotees go to the Ganga or some other sacred river for this festival, in Mauritius all devotees converge to the one and only place, Grand Bassin. It is a crater lake in the heart of the dense forests on the highlands of the island. The pilgrimage may last from one to five days depending upon the length of the journey from the pilgrims' residence to Grand Bassin.

On their return from pilgrimage, devotees congregate in large crowds at the *shivalas* or in marquees put up for the purpose. They spend the nights discoursing, meditating and hymning praises in honour of Shiva. To some who have been tired and exhausted these spots serve as resting places to store energy for onward journey. The pilgrimage has to be completed before the *Shivaratri* night as the water brought from the sacred lake has to be offered to the Lord for the *puja* on this night.

वन्दे देवमुमापतिं सुरगुरुं वन्दे जगत्कारणम् ।
वन्दे पन्नग भूषणम् मृगधरम् वन्दे पशूनां पतिम् ।
वन्दे सूर्य शशांक वह्नि नयनं वन्दे मुकुन्दप्रियम् ।
वन्दे भक्तजनाश्रयं च वन्दे शिव शंकरम् ॥

*Vandé devamumaapatim
sura gurum
Vandé jagat kaaranam
Vandé pannag bhooshanam
mrigadharam
Vandé pashoonaam patim.*

*Vandé soorya shashaanka
vahninayanam
Vandé mukunda priyam.
Vandé bhakta janaashrayam
cha varadam
Vandé shivam shankaram.*

Ganga Talao

Grand Bassin used to be called *Pari Talao* (*pari* - fairies, *talao* - lake) by the first Indian immigrants who came to Mauritius as indentured labourers. In 1897 Shri Jhummun Giri Gossagne, an immigrant from the north east of India who settled as *pujari* (priest) at Terre Rouge had a dream one night. He saw that a lake in the southern part of Mauritius was linked underway to the river Ganga in India. The dream coming from a *pujari*, whose words and views would never be allowed to go untrusted, inspired the community. The followers soon set out on their long and arduous voyage in search of the lake. After untold hardships and struggle through the dense forests they spotted the lake, Grand Bassin. They named it *Pari Talao* , a lake, they concluded, where fairies called at night to bathe, sing and dance.

Years after, in 1972, from rituals performed by the Hindu Maha Sabha, an organisation for the promotion of cultural, social and religious needs of the Hindu Community, the name underwent a change. Water from the sacred river Ganga, symbol of purity and divinity, was brought by the organisation. Following an impressive ceremony the holy water was poured into the lake. The lake was now ritually connected to the divine Ganga, and the investiture resulted in henceforth calling the lake *Ganga Talao*. The lake has further been enhanced with the setting up of new temples and shrines during the past few years by other bodies. The Mauritiuseswar Nath Shiv Jyotir Lingum Mandir is one striking example.

Origin of the festival

The festival has its origin from Shiva's throat which became blue as a result of having swallowed poison coming out from the churning of the sea, and also from Shiva's *Jyotirlinga*.

Nilkanth

Once the *devas* (gods) and the *asuras* (demons) decided to undertake jointly the task of churning the ocean (*sagarmanthan*) to draw out ambrosia by taking which they would become immortal. As it was a colossal task Vishnu intervened to help by supporting the Mount Mandara which was used as the churning rod. The serpent Ananta served as the rope. While they were churning the sea thirteen objects came out. And among them, the ambrosia which however was accompanied by a lethal poison. The poison, on its course, threatened to destroy everything to ashes. Everybody got scared. The *devas* begged Shiva to stop the course. Compassionate as He was, He swallowed the poison. But in the process His throat became blue. The gods, to relieve Him of the heat and pain, poured water on His head. Devotees of Shiva, taking to this belief pour water on Him on *Shivaratri day*, and at any such time they do His *puja*. Since then He came to be popularly known as *Nilkanth* - the blue-throated God.

The Linga

It was the era between the lifeless interval of the dissolution and the creation of the Universe. Vishnu was on his serpent couch floating over the primeval waters when He saw Brahma coming. Brahma was surprised to see Vishnu, as He claimed that nothing could originate without His creation. The creative aspect was Brahma's right, and His alone. A conflict arose between the two concerning as to who should have precedence over the other. As the argument went on endlessly a strong burning light came out of a big *linga,* and stretched from the fathomless limpid water of the ocean to the limitless height of the heaven. Brahma and Vishnu were stunned and came to an agreement. They decided that the one who would be able to ascertain the ends of the light would be given precedence.

Brahma climbing his swan took the flight to the heavens while Vishnu taking the form of a boar (*bara*) dived deep into the ocean. As they proceeded on their way the light grew longer and longer, and the ends seem to be as remote as ever. Exhausted they gave up the search. The *linga* then burst open and from it appeared Shiva. The latter informed them that He was the Progenitor - the Supreme who was the Creator, the Preserver and the Destructor.

Shiva however unhesitatingly shared the title with Brahma and Vishnu, - Brahma being the Creator, Vishnu the Preserver and Himself the Destroyer. The *linga* is said to be constituted in three segments - the lower part representing Brahma, the middle Vishnu, and the top Shiva. This confirms the view that all three are always together.

The law was formulated since that day that Shiva should be worshipped in his phallic form (generator of life process), and not in anthromorphic form (human). Devotees pour water on the *linga* to worship him. In every temple a *lota* (pot) is hung overhead with a tiny hole at the bottom to allow water to fall by droplets on the *linga* throughout day and night.

Shiva Linga

A slight variation to the above legend is that when the five headed Brahma was coming back from the heavens after His unsuccessful attempt. He met the flower *ketaki* (*pandanas odoratissimum*). He contrived with *ketaki* to lie to Vishnu as to having been able to reach the end of the light. Just as Brahma was about to lie, taking *ketaki* as witness, Shiva appeared from the light. He is said to have burnt the head that lied through His third eye, leaving Brahma with only four heads ever since. He cursed *ketaki* so that it would never be accepted in any of his *pujas*. However Brahma implored to Shiva for forgiveness, and Shiva granted him the boon that He would be remembered first in any *hawan* (fire worship). Thus any *hawan* is started by invoking Brahma "*Om Brambhane Namaha*" and the first three sticks immersed in ghee are offered in the fire in His honour. However here again there is some variation as to the punishment inflicted by Shiva. It is said that He was cursed as not to have a cult, temple or festival of His own. Indeed this seems to bear more weight as we do see that Brahma does not seem to enjoy the same favour as Vishnu and Shiva in the triad - Brahma, Vishnu and Mahesh.

29

Puja

The *Shivaratri puja* is usually held at the *shivalas*, and consists of rather elaborate rituals with a wide range of offerings. It is known as the *char pahar ke puja* (the four watches of the night) when rituals are performed at four specific times of the night. The rituals take place (1) sometime before midnight, (2) at midnight (*madyaratri*), (3) sometime after midnight and (4) before dawn. The rituals are in keeping with the *sorahso pachar pujanam*. The important feature of the rituals is the *abhisek*. This involves giving the *linga* successive baths among others with the following (i) milk, (ii) curd, (iii) honey, (iv) ghee, (v) sugar, (vi) fruit juice, (vii) coconut milk, (viii) gold water and (ix) *Gangajal*. Each bath with the objects mentioned is followed by a bath with *soudh* (clean and unpolluted) water. The pilgrims too offer the water brought from the *Ganga Talao* to the *linga* at the time of giving the baths. Finally there is the *maha snaan* with *soudh* water again so as to get the *linga* spotlessly clean. The *linga* is then dressed in new clothing. Betel and *bilwa* leaves are offered by placing them on and around the *linga*, followed by the usual offerings like flowers, in particular the *madar*, sundry fruits, *soupari*, *chandan* paste and *durva* grass. *Mantras* are chanted throughout the rituals. The Shiva *Panchaakshar Mantra* "*Om Namah Shivaya*" is recited 108 times using the *jap mala*. The rituals are closed by having a *hawan* (fire sacrifice). A popular *mantra* for Shiva is the *Mrityum Jaya Mantra* -

> "*Om trayambakam yajaamahe sugandhim pushtivardhanam
> Urvaarukamiva bandhanaan mrityor muksheeya maamritaat.*"

The same rituals are repeated for all the *pujas* at the different times during the night. Throughout the night discourses and recitations from the *Shiv Purana* are held. Hymns such as the *Shiv Tandava Stotrum* and *Shiv Mahima Stotra* are sung. *Bhajans* and *kirtans* to the accompaniment of music are a common feature. The ceremony at the last quarter of the night is closed by the *purnahuti*. With all the rituals completed devotees partake the *prasad* and leave for home.

" I bow down to that three-eyed Lord Shiva, who is full of sweet fragrance, who nourishes the human beings. May He free me from the bondage of Samsara and death, just as a ripe cucumber fruit is separated from the the creeper May I be fixed in immortality."

Lakshmi Ashtami

श्री लक्ष्मी करोतु कल्याणं
आरोग्यं सुख संपदा ।
मम शत्रु विनाशाय दीप ज्योतिर्नमोऽस्तुते ॥

*Lakshmee karotu kalyaanam
Aarogyam sukhasampdam
Mamashtru vinaashaaya
dipa jyotir namostuté.*

Lakshmi Ashtami is the birthday anniversary of Goddess Lakshmi, and is held on the *asthami* (eighth day) in the bright fortnight(*suklapaksh*) of *Phalguna* (February/March). She is the spouse of Vishnu, and the Goddess of Wealth and Beauty. She is usually seen either sitting or standing on a lotus, and has four arms. She holds a lotus in each of the two upper hands, coins flow out from the third hand and with the last hand She gives Her blessings. In some pictures She may be seen holding other objects like the *padma* (lotus), *sankha* (conch), *amritakalasa* (pot of ambrosia), and *bilwa* fruit. These stand for Her power to grant the four *purusarthas* (ends of human life) which are *dharma* (righteousness), *artha* (wealth), *kama* (pleasures of life) and *moksha* (beautitude). It is worthy to note the order of the attributes of the *purusarthas*. One has to live righteously and earn the wealth through the right means. He then enjoys life with that wealth in the right way, and finally works hard to attain *moksha* in the end. When in the company of Her spouse Vishnu, She is usually seen with only two arms.

Lakshmi Narayan

Lakshmi Narayan

Lakshmi has become a very popular deity most probably because of the underlying human desire for wealth and beauty. However this is only a partial meaning of Her attributes. Indeed what one would need to seek is spiritual enlightenment. She is often seen together with Lord Vishnu who is invested with the qualities of permanence and perseverance. Whenever Lord Vishnu has taken any *awatar* She has incarnated beside Him. She appeared as Sita when Vishnu incarnated as Rama, as Dharani when He came as Parashurama, as Radha in His Krishna *awatar*. Because of their togetherness the couple is known as *Lakshmi Narayan.* And since a female deity manifests Herself as the active power (*shakti*) of Her counterpart, worshipping and invoking the blessings of the two together gives an added measure of conviction of prayers being responded to more favourably and with long-lasting effect. Indeed while one is the bestower of wealth the other is the preserver of that wealth The special offering to Mother Lakshmi is the *pooah* made of flour and sugar.

The *Bhagavat Purana* mentions that Lakshmi appeared when the *devas* (minor gods) and the demons were churning the ocean (*samamanthan*) in a bid to draw out the elixir of immortality. Lord Vishnu, incarnating as a tortoise, supported Mount Mandara which was being used as the churning rod, and the huge serpent Vasuki (Ananta) served as the rope. In the process thirteen precious objects came out, and among them Lakshmi. The objects were shared among all those who were involved in the task. Lakshmi was taken by Vishnu. An allegory to the above is that when one's mind is churned by divine thoughts and meditation spiritual wealth pours out that leads him to the doorstep of the Almighty.

Mother Lakshmi

Varalakshmi

Another festival which is linked with Lakshmi is the *Varalakshmi puja* which is more commonly celebrated in Karnataka and Maharashtra, in India. The goddess is famous for granting boons (*varas*) particularly of security and protection, and Her *puja* is considered to be very auspicious for married women. A legend would have it that Lakshmi was very fond of worshipping Shiva. She used to pray and offer Him one thousand lotus buds daily. One day the buds fell short by two. Lakshmi recalling that Her consort Lord Vishnu used to compare Her breasts to lotus buds, cut them off to make the number. Just then Shiva manifested Himself. Highly pleased with Her sacrifice and devotion, He blessed Her, and informed Her that the cut breasts would blossom into the sacred *bilva* (*Aegle marmelos*) tree and whose leaves would be offered to Him on all auspicious occasions.

Sometimes we see Ganesha together with Lakshmi. The interpretation is that Lakshmi is the bestower of wealth and beauty, but without the support of knowledge and wisdom these two attributes are not likely to perform fully. Hence the presence of Ganesha, the Lord of Wisdom, who by bestowing knowledge enables the devotee to make the best use of his wealth and beauty.

Holi

Holi-Ho! Holi-Ho! fills the air. It is the *pratipada* (first day) of the dark fortnight (*krishnapaksh*) of the month of *Chaitra* (March/April) and it is *Holi*. The mood is jubilant. The festival calls for celebration in all its splendour, and in frenzy too in the *phagua* spirit.

Indeed the preparations for the celebration of the colourful festival of *Holi* start just after the *Vasant Panchami*. In the past, on this very day, an announcement popularly known as *"tal thonkagal "* used to be made in *shivalas*, *baitkas* or at public gatherings to inform people that *phagua* was on the heels. Everybody had to be ready for the celebration of the festival. The *Holika Dahan* is held on the eve which is the *purnima* (full moon day) of the month of *Phalguna* (February/March). As one would see, the festival takes two days for its observance.

Spirit of Holi

Holi is celebrated in almost all parts of India, though with much more fervour in the north where the celebration may last several days. At this time of the year the crops have been harvested, the barns and granaries are full, the toil is over. Man now needs to relax and enjoy the fruits of his labour. He needs to be supplied with the tonic to cheer him up and restore his peace of mind. Here comes *Holi* to provide him with joy and new life, to inspire him with hope, to free himself. As it is spring, many of the gardens and the fields are in bloom, the trees are laden with flowers with bees hovering over them in quest of honey. The lakes are crowded with lovely birds warbling and dancing in a variety of ways. The forests and mountains are rippling with charm. Nature unfolds itself and is a picture of felicity. Although the season is different in Mauritius and the climate is hot , yet the fervour is all the same as traditions have been kept alive.

The festival is celebrated by sprinkling coloured water, sometimes using *pichkaris* (syringes) on family members, relatives, friends, passers-by and almost anybody one comes across.

Many use the *gulal* (dried coloured powder) instead to smear faces and bodies of members of the family and other people. It is the day when all inimical feelings are buried, giving way to vows and promises of renewed friendship and love. Inhibitions are shed away for feelings of freedom and gay abandon. The coloured water is sprinkled with great rejoicing on one another,

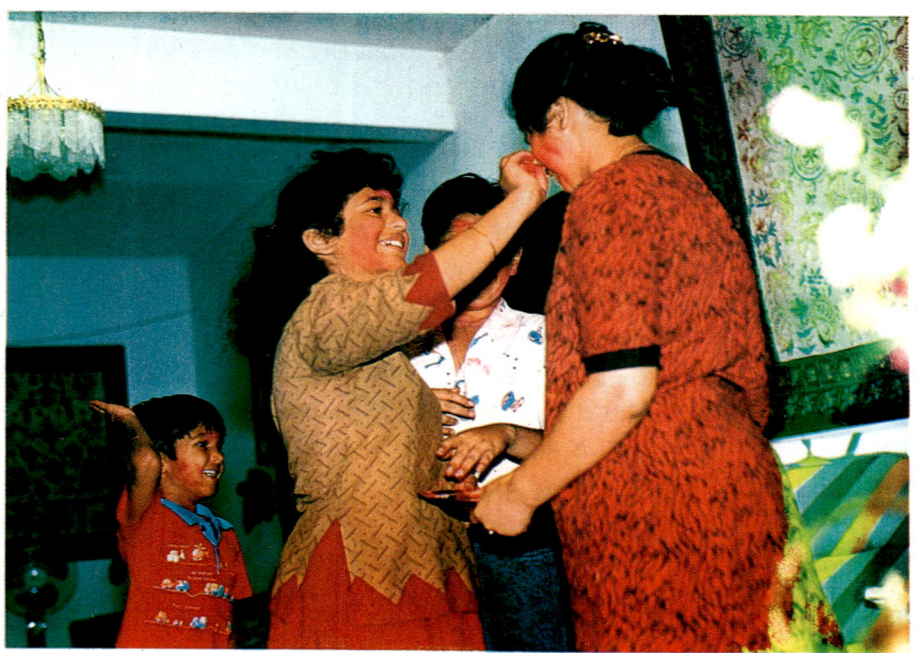
Celebrating Holi

Everybody feels happy. Be it at home or outside, in the office or in the market place, on the bus or in the field, man opens out to himself. He sings, he shouts and he dances. Certain liberties are even taken. Groups while singing even take some *bhang*, an intoxicating drink. It is said that in some tribal communities in India, *Holi* being a relic of primitive fertility rite, drinking bouts and sex orgies take place and are even condoned by society in the spirit of *Holi*.

Origin of the festival

Although agrarian in origin, the festival also draws sustenance from mythological legends. The most popular is the one connected with the demon king Hiranyakashyapu. From severe penances performed, he had obtained a boon from Brahma that he could not be killed either by beast or man, either during the day or during the night, either inside a building or outside. This boon convinced him that he was invincible, and as the days went by his pride swelled and along with it his cruelty and wickedness. He mistook himself for the Supreme Being. He ordered all his subjects to pray him and owe allegiance to him, and him alone. However his son Prahlad who had been imbued with the love of God while still in the womb of his mother openly defied him. Prahlad's refusal to abide by his order angered the king who devised several means, such as pushing him down high cliffs or closing him in dens with dangerous beasts, to have him killed. But each time he came out safe, and with stronger faith in the Lord.

The king had a sister Holika who had got the boon that she could not be burnt by fire. She proposed to sit with Prahlad on a blazing fire, with the thought that the child would get burnt to ashes and herself coming out safe. As usual the Lord protected Prahlad, and Holika was burnt instead. As for the king when his cruelty and wickedness became unbearable, the Lord appeared one day at dusk from a pillar in the palace as *Narsingh* (man-lion). He dragged him to the doorstep and killed him there, thus safeguarding the vow that he was not killed either by man or beast, either during the day or at night, and either inside a building or outside. An effigy is burnt on the eve in remembrance of Holika, whence the name of *Holi* given to the festival. The next day is the day of rejoicing for having got rid of Holika and the demon king Hiranyakashyapu.

Another legend regarding the burning of effigies on the eve is associated with the death of Putana. Kansa, the evil king of Mathura, was cursed to be destroyed by his sister's son Krishna. The king, to save himself, devised several ways to have Krishna killed. One of them was to have him suckle from the poisonous breasts of the demoness Putana. One day Putana called at Gokula and lulled Krishna into suckling from her breast. Krishna sucked so hard that she was drained of her very life. Hence the burning of the effigy of Putana.

Another legend connected with the burning of effigy is related to Agni. The *rishi* Bhrigu was married to a very beautiful woman called Puloma. One day he requested the deity Agni, to whom he offered oblations daily, to keep watch over his spouse, and protect her against the *asuras* during his absence. While the *rishi* was away, Agni allowed himself to be lured by the *asuras* who abducted Puloma. On his return, Bhrigu, angry at not seeing his wife pronounced a curse on Agni that he would henceforth be fed with only useless and soiled objects. Agni appealed to Lord Vishnu who intervened on his behalf to Bhrigu and the punishment was reduced to one day in a year. Hence the bonfire on the *Holika Dahan* when all useless objects are burnt.

Celebrating the festival

In the preceding days of the festival devotees clean their houses, making them bright and cheerful. They remove all dirty and useless articles and burn them. As with all the Hindu festivals, devotees wake up early. After taking a bath, they prepare themselves for *puja*. All members of the family recite prayers and worship the idols of their preferred gods with offerings like *prasad* (cereals cooked in milk),fruit, flowers and holy basil leaves The most striking feature is the use of *abir* (coloured powder) which is mixed with water. The coloured water is first applied as a *tika* on the forehead of each of the idols. Lord Shiva, and Lord Vishnu in His incarnations as Krishna and Rama, are worshipped. After the *puja* the coloured water, now prepared in large quantities and, with the use of *pichkaris* (syringes) is sprayed on all members of the family with great rejoicing. A mood of fulfilment prevails and everybody participates in the celebration. Nobody is spared and even passers-by, visitors and pets are drenched with the coloured water. It is taken in good spirit.

The festival usually ends by midday but in some cases the celebration is stretched till the evening. Groups assembled in *baitkas* or special places perform a *yajna* (fire sacrifice) and offer prayers. They bake cakes, the most popular of which is the *pooah* made, among other things, with flour, milk, sugar, and dried grapes. They also prepare the cherished drink of the day - the *bhang*. When the rituals are over and the *prasad* is partaken they give themselves to mirth and merriment. They sing to the music of *jhal* (cymbals), *dholak* (drum) and other musical instruments. Holi songs are rendered in all their splendour, and the rendering becomes more soul stirring under the spell of an increasing dose of the *bhang*. However one should not get away with the idea that the rejoicings are an end in themselves. They have a spiritual significance as through them man is eventually weaned away from sensual pleasures and gradually taken to the spiritual path since all the bits and pieces of the rejoicings are linked to the divine.

Nav Varsh

Nav Varsh is the New Year day and is celebrated on the *pratipada* (first day) of the bright fortnight (*suklapaksh*) of the month of *Chaitra* (March/April). The reckoning of the years according to the Indian system is done by what is known as the *samvatsar*. The *samvatsar* cycle spans over a period of sixty years. This duration is split into three parts called *binshas* each of twenty years in honour of the triad - Brahma, Vishnu, and Rudra

Brahma	**Vishnu**	**Rudra**
1. Prabhavah	21. Sarvajitt	41. Plavangha
2. Vibhavah	22. Sarvadhari	42. Kilakaha
3. Shuklaha	23. Virodhi	43. Sawmyaha
4. Pramodaha	24. Vikrashi	44. Sadharanaha
5. Prajapati	25. Kharaha	45. Virodhkritt
6. Anguiraha	26. Nandanaha	46. Paridhavi
7. Shrimukha	27. Vijayaha	47. Pramadi
8. Bhavaha	28. Jayaha	48. Anandaha
9. Yuva	29. Manmathaha	49. Rakcchasaha
10. Dhata	30. Durmukhaha	50. Nalaha
11. Ishwarah	31. Hemlambi	51. Pingalaha
12. Bahudhanayaha	32. Vikrambi	52. Kaalyuktaha
13. Pramathi	33. Vikari	53. Siddharthi
14. Vikramaha	34. Shaarvari	54. Rawdraha
15. Vryshha	35. Plavaha	55. Durmatiha
16. Chitrabhanuha	36. Subhakrit	56. Dundubhi
17 Subhanuha	37. Shobhanaha	57. Rudhirodgaari
18. Taranha	38. Krodhi	58. Raktakshi
19. Parthivaha	39. Vishwavasuha	59. Krodhanaha
20 Vyayaha	40. Parabhadaha	60. Akshaya

The first twenty years constitute the Brahma *binsha*, next is the Vishnu *binsha*, and last the Rudra *binsha*. Then each year (*samvatshar*) in every *binsha* is given a name. For example the year 1995 is in the *Vishnu binsha* and the year is *sarvadhari*.

During the preceding days of the *Nav Varsh* the yard, the house, and almost all corners are given a thorough cleaning. The *puja ghar* is given particular attention. The idols are ceremoniously bathed and donned with new clothing. Some have a *kalash sthapna* as the day also marks the beginning of the *Navratri* period. Special offerings are made and prayers chanted.

A year in the Indian calendar is reckoned to have twelve months each of thirty days or *tithis*. The month is accounted on the cycle of the moon and is divided into two *pakshas* (fortnights) of 15 days each, the *krishnapaksh* (dark fortnight) and the *suklapaksh* (bright fortnight). In the Indian calendar the month begins with the first day of the *krishnapaksh* and ends with the last day, the *purnima* (full moon) of the *suklapaksh*. The moon affords convenient punctuations to decide on the days to hold festivals.

According to the lunar months the year consists of about 354 solar days only, as the 30 lunar days of each month make for only 29 1/2 solar days. To make up for the shortage, an *adhikmas* (additional) month is accounted after every 30 lunar months. This leap month occurs usually after *Ashada* (June/July) or *Shravana* (July/August), making that year one of thirteen months instead of twelve. There is also a difference between the Gregorian and the Indian calendar. The lunar month in the Indian calendar begins on or about the 21st day of the corresponding month in the Gregorian calendar, e.g. the first day of *Chaitra* would be around the 21st of March. The year 1995 in the Gregorian calendar is the year 2052 in the Indian calendar.

New Year Day

There are differences in the practices of the reckoning of New Year Day by the various sects in India. Some have calculations according to the solar system, and others according to the lunar system. As a result distinctive differences occur in the months and the dates. There is the Telugu New Year, the Tamil New Year, and seemingly a different New Year for the North Indians. In some communities the *Maha Sankranti* or the *Pongal* is considered as the beginning of the year, in others the first day of the *Navratri* in *Chaitra,* and still in others the *Divali*.

Months of the Year

The months of the *Vikram Samvat* corresponding to the months in the Gregorian calendar are thus - *Chaitra* - March/April, *Vaishaka* - April/May, *Jyeshtha* - May/June, *Ashadha* - June/July, *Shravana* - July/August, *Bhadrapad* - August/September, *Ashvina*- September/October, *Kartika* - October/November, *Agrahana/Maghiis* - November/December, *Pausha* - December / January, *Magha* - January/February, *Phalguna* - February/March.

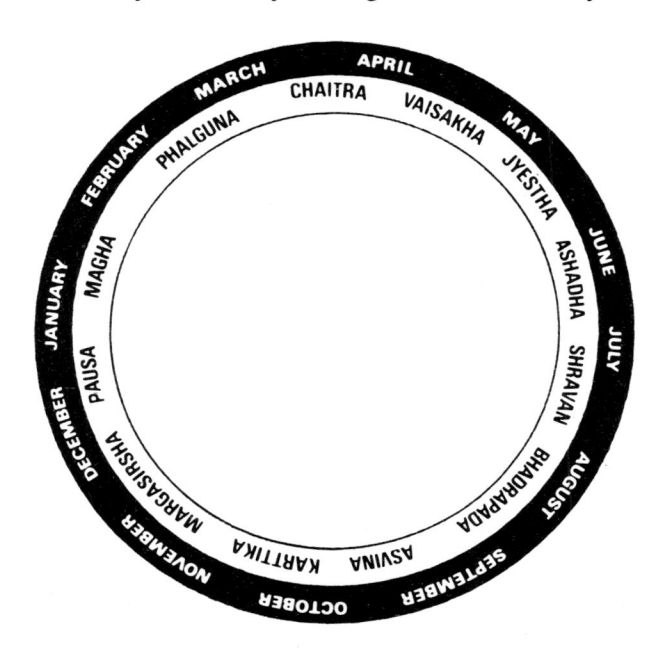

The lunar months

Days and the deities worshipped -

Day	Name	Planet	Deities
Sunday	**Ravivar**	**Sun**	**Surya, Saraswati**
Monday	**Somvaar/ Chandravaar**	**Moon**	**Shiva, Chandra**
Tuesday	**Mangalvaar/ Bhaumbar/ Kujvaar**	**Mars**	**Hanuman, Durga Kartike**
Wednesday	**Bhoodhvaar**	**Mercury**	**Vishnu, Ganesha, Krishna, Rama**
Thursday	**Guruvaar/ Brihaspativaar**	**Jupiter**	**Durga, Guru, Saraswati**
Friday	**Shukravaar/ Briguvaar**	**Venus**	**Kali, Durga, Lakshmi, Indra**
Saturday	**Shanivaar**	**Saturn**	**Hanuman, Sanidev**

Rama Navmi

Rama Navmi marks the birth anniversary of God Rama who is the seventh incarnation of Lord Vishnu. The *Rama Navmi* period starts on the first lunar day of the bright fortnight (*suklapaksh*) of the month of *Chaitra* (March/April) and spreads over a period of nine days. The ninth day is the birthday of Lord Rama. In fact the *Rama Navmi* is the *Durga Navratri* period when Mother Durga and the other goddesses Kali, Lakshmi and Saraswati are worshipped. Since Lord Rama was born during this time on the ninth day the festival is commonly known as *Rama Navmi*. He prayed to Mother Durga for nine days before being able to defeat the demon king Ravana on the tenth day. The *Navratri* is observed twice a year, once in the month of *Chaitra* (March/April), the other in the month of *Asvina* (September/October). Some devotees in India and Mauritius hold a *Navaratri* puja four times a year.

The first day of the *Navaratri* is considered as the beginning of the year, or of the era itself. It is believed that the universe was created on this day by Brahma. At the beginning of time, if time it can be called, there was only the Supreme Self-existing Maha Vishnu. He split himself into three bodies - Brahma, Vishnu and Mahesh. The task of creating the universe was entrusted to Brahma, that of preserving to Vishnu and of destruction to Shiva. Legends vary as to the creation of the world. According to one legend Brahma created the waters of the earth and deposited a seed which became the golden egg. He took birth out of it Himself. In due course He produced a daughter, Vach, by whom He fathered all creatures. Another legend mentions that Brahma became a boar and raised the earth from the primaeval waters and created the universe. Yet another legend assumes that He came as a fish or a tortoise to create the world.

नीलाम्बुजश्यामल कोमालांग
सीता समारोपित वाम भागम् ।
पाणै महा सायक चारू चापं
ननामि रामं रघुवंश नाथम् ॥

Neelaambhuja syaamala komalaangam
Seetaa samaaropita vaamabhaagam.
Paanau mahaa saayaka chaaru chaapam
Namaami raamamraghu vanshanaatham.

Origin of Rama's Birth

The legends as to Lord Rama's incarnation are several. The first one is connected with the demon king Ravana. Lord Vishnu had two favourite gate-keepers, Jaya and Vijaya. Due to a curse pronounced on them by the Brahman Sanaka and his brothers they had to take birth thrice as demons. In the first birth they came as the demons Hiranyakashyapa and Hiranyakashyapu. The Lord took *avatara* as *Vamana* (boar) to kill Hiranyakashya and as a *Narsingh* (man-lion) to kill Hiranyakashyapu. Next they were born as Ravana and Kumbakarana, and it is then that the Lord incarnated as Rama. Finally they came as Sisupala and Dantavakra and were killed by Krishna.

Another reason is that the Lord had to suffer Sage Narada's curse. Narada was once in a trance in a cave on the Himayalas. The God of Love, Kamadeva, at the request of Indra, tried to seduce him through his *maya* (illusive power) but failed. Narada acquired a pride for his success over the God of Love. He went to boast of himself to Shiva who warned him not to reveal his feelings of self-esteem to anybody. But Narada's pride swelled all the more in response to this warning. He next called on Lord Vishnu and made an *exposé* of his success. Seeing him puffed up with pride, the Lord devised a means to cure him of the disease. He spread His *maya* over him. He created a fake city with a glorious king holding a *swayambar* for his lovely daughter. Narada reached the spot, and was so struck by her beauty that he rushed to Lord Vishnu and begged for His beauty. Instead the Lord made a mockery of him and gave him the face of a monkey. He sat proudly at the princely gathering hoping to be garlanded as the choicest bridegroom. Seeing the princess's indifference and hearing about the mockery his appearance elicited from other participants he rushed to look at himself in the mirror. He flew into a temper at seeing himself. He hastened to the Lord and in great anger cursed Him -

> **"Smitten with pangs of separation from your wife**
> **You will need the help of monkeys to recover Her."**

When the Lord withdrew the charm of His *maya*, Narada came to himself. Locked up in repentance he begged the Lord for forgiveness, and for the curse to be ineffectual. However God, upholder of truth and righteousness would not alter the course.

Once the sage Gautama went away and left his wife Ahilya alone in the hermitage. Lord Indra disguising himself as her husband Gautama approached her and lured her into an amorous adventure. The sage came to know about it. On his return he cursed her in most hideous terms and reduced her to a big lifeless rock. Ahilya writhing in agony pleaded for forgiveness as she claimed not to be responsible for the infringement. The sage in his state of contrition reduced the punishment by giving her the blessing that she would be redeemed by the Lord in His Rama's incarnation.

Another legend is the one connected with King Pratapabhanu, his brother Arimardanand and their minister Dharmaruchi. Through a curse pronounced on them by the Brahmans they were born as Ravana, Kumbhakaarana and Vibhishana in their subsequent births.

Still another reason for the Lord to incarnate as Rama was for the sake of His devotees Manu and Satrupa. At the close of their reign as king and queen, Manu and Satrupa retired to the forests. They proceeded to Naimisavanya where, with much fervour and devotion listened to the sacred scriptures, the *Puranas*, in the company of sages. In complete surrender and love for the Lord they set on an endless voyage of penance, and *japa* - *"Om Namo Bhagawate Vasudevaya."* Pleased with their devotion and love the Lord manifested before them. The couple stunned with trancendental love gazed on Him with unblinking eyes. They were lost in the manifestation and beauty of the Lord. When they were awakened the Lord offered to confer a boon on them -

" *O king, ask of Me unreservedly; there is nothing which I would not give.*"

The couple enamoured of the Lord and His beauty requested that they should be endowed with a son like Him. To have another Being like Himself was next to impossible. He offered Himself to be their son in their next birth.

" *Amen ! But where shall I go to find My equal ?
I Myself, O King shall be a son to you.*"

The couple came as Dasratha and Kaushalya, King and Queen of Ayodhya. He was born as their son Rama.

Rama's Avatar

Ravana took birth as the demon king of Lanka. In response to his penance and devotion to Lord Shiva he was conferred the boon of being almost invincible. His might and self-esteem convinced him of his superiority over all beings and gods. As a result he became wicked and ruthless, and would not allow any religious ceremony or spiritual observance. He committed endless misery to gods, sages and human beings alike. They were all terror striken and miserable. Consequently they repaired to Lord Vishnu accompanied by Mother Earth, Brahma and Shiva. After listening to them the Lord reassured them and informed that He would soon be incarnating as Rama, son of King Dasratha and Queen Kaulshalya who had already taken birth in Ayodhya.

King Dasaratha was married since long and was yet childless. One day he called on Sage Vasistha and expressed his wish of having a heir to his throne. The sage summoned Sage Sringhi and a *yajna* (sacrifice) was performed. While the king was offering oblations into the sacred fire, the Fire-God appeared with an offering of *khir* (rice boiled in milk) as *prasad*. He was asked to share it among his three queens. The king gave half of the offering to Queen Kaulshalya. He then divided the remaining half into two parts, one of which was taken by his queen Kaikeyi. The remaining was again split into two parts and placed in the hands of Kaulshalya and Kaikeyi to be handed over to the third queen Sumitra. Soon all the queens became pregnant, and joy and prosperity spread over the kingdom. The time was being happily spent till the auspicious time came for the Lord to reveal Himself -

As a forerunner to the auspicious event *nagas*, sages and gods appeared and offerred hymns of praises. The Lord of the Universe and the solace of all creation now manisfested Himself before His mother, Queen Kaulshalya. He appeared in his All glorious form as He had presented Himself to her and her husband in their previous births as Manu and Satrupa. The mother on seeing Him was stunned and extolled His glory -

> *" O infinite Lord, how can I praise you ! The Vedas as well as the Puranas declare You as transcending Maya, beyond attributes, above knowledge and beyond all measure. He who is sung by the Vedas and holy men as an ocean of mercy and bliss and the repository of all virtues, the same Lord of Laksmi, the lover of His devotees, has revealed Himself for my good. "*

The Lord was born. Dasaratha and all were drowned in ecstasy and bliss on seeing the peerless baby. Alongside, Queen Kaikeyi gave birth to her son Bharata, and Sumitra to her two sons Lakshmana and Shatrughna. The joy and grandeur of the occasion was past all telling. Showers of flowers dropped from heaven; everybody was rapt in the joy of absorption into Brahma. The occasion defied description. Lord Shiva Himself could not help not to be present on the occasion -

> *"O Girja, the sage Kakabhusundi and Myself both were there together in human form without anyone knowing it. Elated with supreme joy and the delight of love we roamed about the streets in ecstasy forgetting ourselves. He alone who enjoyed Shri Rama's grace could be apprised of this blessed adventure of ours"*

The Puja

During the *Navmi* period and up to the full moon day of this bright fortnight, *pujas* are performed in honour of Goddesses Durga, Kali, Lakshmi, and Saraswati in addition to Lord Rama. The house, in particular the *puja ghar*, is thoroughly cleaned. The idols are wiped cleaned and donned with new clothes. Devotees keep to a strict disciplined life of celibacy and austerity. Some go on a thorough light sweet meal, others have only one meal a day. Though others take all their meals yet they completely abstain from non-vegetable dishes and alcoholic drinks.

Devotees make a *kalash*, just as they make one for the *Durga Navmi puja* in the month of *Ashvina*. They have a dried coconut to which they give all facial traits. The coconut is placed on a pot and adorned, so that when all is set, the whole arrangement gives the look of a serene lady in a sitting position. Every morning and evening rituals are performed with offerings.

During these days devotees congregate in large groups till late in the night at the *shivalas*. Recitations and discourses from the scriptures, mostly from the *Ramayana* and the *Devi Mahatyam* are held. On the ninth day morning devotees throng to the *shivalas* with special offerings to worship the Lord. Special rituals are held. A cradle is made and the idol of Rama as a baby is placed in. The cradle is beautifully decorated, the baby is garlanded and revered as a holy guest. At noon devotees, mostly ladies, swing the cradle singing lullabies and dancing round it. And when all is over *prasad* is distributed to the devotees.

Shri Ram liye awatar
surem harassayi
Anand bhadaiyi awadh puri
Sakhyen mangal gawé
Kahé Mahadeo Parvati sé
Sakhian mangal gawé.

The kalash

Ram Rajya

Tulsidas has beautifully portrayed Lord Rama in his *Ramcharit Manas* and every line of the epic fills the mind with wonder and and nectar of bliss. It is really next to impossible to find a parallel to the character of Lord Rama. He excelled Himself as a man, son, brother, husband, father or king. Kind and sweet in speech, courteous and handsome in appearance, He was the embodiment of excellence and perfection. He possessed an unusual depth of sensibility for peace, goodness and harmony. He was full of grace which brought all His citizens together and reconciled their differences. He spoilt His subjects who were utterly devoted to Him. They loved Him, and were happy, fearless and unaffected. His love and sense of dedication to the welfare, happiness and prosperity of His subjects made of Him a most cherished monarch. He took birth for the cause of *dharma.* Truth, goodness and righteousness found their fullest expression in His kingdom, and the *Ram Rajya* has ever since been the dream of every citizen.

"Rama raj baithem trailoka
Harashit bhae gae sab soka"

Hanuman Jayanti

Hanuman Jayanti is the birthday anniversary of Lord Hanuman, the son of Vayu, the Wind-God. It is held on the *purnima* (full moon day) of the brigh half (*suklapaksh*) of *Chaitra* (March/April). Hanuman is a very popular deity and most Hindus keep an image of him in their *puja ghar* (prayer room), and a shrine is built in his honour in a corner of the yard. The shrine has usually very high bamboo masts with red flags at the top. It is the practice to light an earthen lamp in the shrine before dusk time everyday. Some people consider that Hanuman was born on the *chaturdashi* (fourteenth day) of the dark fortnight (*krishnapaksh*) of *Kartika* (October/November), that is on the *Narak Chaturdashi Yam* day.

In complete surrender

His image

Hanuman is found in several postures but two of them are most common. When portrayed alone he is seen with a mace in his right hand, and upholding a mountain in his left hand. Rama's brother, Lakshmana, was once struck by an arrow shot by Meghnath, Ravana's son, during the fight between Rama and Ravana. He lay unconcious. The *Ved* (doctor) prescribed healing herbs which were to be found only on the Himalaya mountains and had to be brought to him before dawn the next day. Hanuman flew from Lanka in the south, and crossed over the whole country to reach Himalaya in the north. Not being able to identify the herbs, he uprooted the mountain and brought it to the *Ved*. It is believed that Hanuman caught and held the Sun in his custody the whole night, and released him only after the herbs were applied to Lakshmana. Hence the portrayal of him with a mountain.

The other posture is that when he is in the company of Lord Rama, Sita and Lakshmana. He is seen in complete and loving surrender at the feet of his master. His long tail, a matter of great pride to him, always loops over his head. His devotion is so great that when once he was put to test, he opened his chest to convince his challengers that his heart was but an abode of the Lord and His consort. He is yellow-bodied, has a red face, wears a red loin cloth and a crown on his head. He is the ubiquitous servant, the epitome of devoted service and loyalty. He is an embodiment of strength and wisdom. He is a great scholar excelling in the scriptures and the sciences, and is the ninth author of grammar.

His Birth

Once a *rishi* was performing penance when he saw a wild elephant coming towards him. He pleaded for protection. Keshari, a man of unequalled strength rushed to the *rishi's* rescue and drove away the animal. The *rishi* was much relieved and felt so contented that he offered to confer a boon upon him. Keshari asked that he should get a son as strong and as swift as the wind. After some time his wife Anjani became pregnant. One day she was resting on a rock when the winds began to blow very fiercely. She felt that she would soon be stripped off of her clothes. Screaming in fury she threatened to curse the Wind-God, Vayu, on the strength of her chastity, as a *sati*. Vayu begged for pardon. He informed her that he was only accomplishing the boon as requested by her husband. By blowing so hard over her body he was just impregnating her son with the strength and speed of the wind. The child when born was known as *Pawan Putra,* the son of the Wind-God.

His prowess

When he was a child, Hanuman mistook the Sun for a ripe fruit. Some say that he was attracted by the redness of the Sun as he was very fond of red. He flew to the heavens. He grasped and swallowed the Sun. Darkness spread everwhere and everybody got frightened. The gods and goddesses pleaded to him. He then released the Sun. It is said that later the Sun sought the help of Hanuman. The Sun had a very wicked and disobedient child called Sani. He was spending his days loitering and gambling. Hanuman took the son to task and brought him to his father. In return the Sun taught the *Jyoti Vidya* to Hanuman.

Hanuman in the service of his Lord

Hanuman had the power to reduce or expand himself to any size and form. Once he was crossing the sea to go to Lanka in search of Mother Sita. Out from the sea appeared a demoness. She wanted to swallow him, thus preventing him to reach Lanka. Hanuman prayed to her, saying that he would surrender himself to her once he would have completed his duty. But since she had vowed of having him in her stomach there and then, she did not give in. To avoid being caught Hanuman expanded himself. And so did the demoness with her mouth. The struggle went on each trying to outdo the other in the task of expanding. Then Hanuman reduced himself to an atom in the twinkling of an eye, entered her mouth and came out. The vow was fulfilled and the demoness allowed him free passage.

Hanuman is very famous for his superhuman powers. His outstanding performance in Lanka deserves mention. After meeting Sita in the Ashoka garden in Lanka Hanuman felt hungry. He started eating the fruits and uprooting the trees. The guards saw him and there followed a fight between him and the demons. Finally after putting up a very tough fight Hanuman allowed himself to be taken prisoner by Ravana's son, Meghnath, who had launched the *brahma shastra* (weapon presided by Brahma). He was brought to the palace of King Ravana where he fell into strong arguments with him. As punishment Ravana and his advisers decided to burn his tail, which is the pride of any monkey. He stretched his tail as bait. The tail, swathed with rags, was soaked in oil and set on fire. By his magical power, Hanuman instantly, reduced himself in size and slipped out of the bonds. He sprang to the attics of the golden palace and other buildings, and burnt Lanka to the ground.

मनोजवं मारुत तुल्य वेगं ।
जितेन्द्रियं बुद्धिमतां वरिष्ठम् ।
वातात्मजं वानर यूथ मुख्यं ।
श्री राम दूतं शरणं प्रपद्ये ॥

The Eternel Youth

When the war between Rama and Ravana was over, Hanuman accompanied Rama to Ayodhya. He stayed there for quite some time. And when the time came for his departure the Lord conferred on him the reward of perpetual youth and strength; and most important the boon that whenever and wherever Rama would be prayed he would along with Him be hymned with praise. The boon of eternal youth, virtue and strength was earlier granted to Hanuman by Sita when he visited her in Lanka -

*Manojavam maaruta tulya végam
Jitendriyam budhimattam varishtham.
Vaataatmajam vaanara yooth mukhyam
Shree raama dootam shranam prapadyé.*

" May you become a repository of strength and virtue, dear child. May you ever remain immune from old age and death, and prove to be a store house of good qualities, my son. and may the Lord of the Raghus shower His abundant grace on you "

The two books *Hanuman Chalissa* and *Hanuman Bahuk* are a living testimony of the greatness and achievements of Hanuman. Many people read the *Hanuman Chalissa* almost daily to be embodied with the same sense of devotion, selflessness and love for the Lord.

Puja

On this day, as for all festivals, people take an early bath and go to the *puja* room which is given a thorough cleaning. All the idols or images are cleaned. The *sohraso pachar pujanam* is performed with welcoming rituals and offerings. The idol of Hanuman is donned with new red clothing, and the *janeo* (sacred thread) is changed. He is garlanded. Betel leaves are spread in front of him, on which flowers, *soopari, chandan paste* and fruits are laid. A coconut, some bananas, *rots* (special cakes made of flour and ghee) and basil leaves are offered. *Sindoor* which is offered to married women only is exceptionally applied to him, he being a celibate. Sandal is lit and *aarti* is done. As Hanuman is a supreme devotee of Lord Rama, excerpts from the *Ramayana* are read, in particular the chapter *Sundarkand*. The *Hanuman Chalissa* and the *Hanuman Sankatmochan* are recited. Some also take this opportunity to perform the *Dhaja puja*. This involves the ceremony according to which the masts and flags at the shrine outside, *Hanuman Chawtra*, are changed. After the *puja* the *prasad* is distributed. Many people go to the *shivalas* on this occasion as all are equipped with an idol of Hanuman.

Mother Sita

Jankee Jayanti

Jankee Jayanti is the birthday anniversary of Sita, daughter of King Janaka and spouse of Lord Rama. This festival is held on the *navmi* (ninth day) in the bright fortnight (*suklapaksh*) of the month of *Vaishaka* (April/May). She is *par excellence* the embodiment of all virtues - love, self-sacrifice and chastity. She is always seen and prayed in company of her Lord. Most of the time sitting on His left she shines resplendent in her exquisite beauty like the bud of a gold lily beside a fresh lotus.

उद्भवस्थिति सहार कारीणी क्लेश हारिणीम् ।
सर्व श्रेयस्करी सीता नताऽह राम वल्लभाम् ॥

Birth

Her birth took place in the city of Janaka. The evil king of Lanka, Ravana, had spread his authority on many cities by subduing their rulers. His influence and wickedness knew no bounds. He had even conquered the gods. His greed for wealth grew as fast and as wide as his authority spread. He started exacting heavy taxes from the conquered kings and gods. Soon the heavy tolls became so unbearable that the taxpayers grew tired of him and sought means to escape from his cruelty.

Each of the taxpayers took some blood from his body and collected it in a vessel impregnated with *mantras*. Once when the soldiers of Ravana called to collect the rates they locked the vessel and handed it over to them. They asked them to inform Ravana that the opening of the vessel would spell doom to his kingdom and himself. Ravana, to protect himself from the curse ordered that the vessel be concealed deep in the ground in King Janaka's land. If any wrong were to happen it would be to King Janaka and not to him.

Some time after, a drought occurred in the city of Janak. The king who was a great devotee of the Lord, underwent vigorous fasting and penance. He was recommended to perform a big religious ceremony (*yajna*) on his land, and it so happened that the place chosen was where the vessel of blood had been buried. Just as they were performing the *yajna*, the vessel sprang up and out of it came a lovely child. She was the embodiment of goodness and beauty. King Janaka took her home as his daughter. He called her Sita, a word meaning furrow. She became the princess Jankee. As she came out of the Earth, she was the child of Mother Earth, and later when the end was imminent she gave herself up to Mother Earth.

The birth of Jankee spelt doom for Ravana later. When he abducted her while she was in exile in the forest, her husband waged war against him and destroyed him. Jankee is the symbol of perfection in all splendour - as a daughter, as a wife, as a daughter-in-law, as a mother and as a queen. One has to see how she abandoned the comfort and warmth of city life to accompany her Lord to the forests. Her behaviour towards Ravana speaks for itself. To prove her chastity and her loyalty for her husband she even stood the ordeal by fire after coming from Lanka where she had been kept as a prisoner. Later once again, she abandoned the palace and separated from her husband to keep her subjects happy. The spirit of sacrifice and duty made of her the gem of womanhood.

Udbhava sthiti sanhaara
Kaarineem klésha harineem
Sarva shréyaskareem seetaam
Natoham raama vallabhaam.

Lord Rama and His consort Sita

On the other hand Rama symbolises the cream of masculine virtues. His fidelity, gentleness and steadfastness have excelled the ideal qualities of manhood. As each of Rama and Sita was the other's only partner, they are looked upon as a striking example of constancy in marriage and affectionate compliance. On this day of the *puja* devotees worship the couple with various offerings. They read from the *Ramayana*, and meet in *satsang* where the glory and merits of both are chanted.

Parvati Jayanti

Parvati is the spouse of Shiva. The festival is held on the *chaturdashi* (fourth day) in the bright fortnight (*suklapaksh*) of the month of *Jyeshtha* (May/June) to celebrate the birthday anniversary of Mother Parvati.

Sati

शिवायै हरकान्तायै प्रकृत्यै सृष्टि हतवे ।
नमस्ते ब्रह्मचारिण्यै जगद्धात्र्यै नमो नमः ।

In Her previous birth, Parvati came as Sati. Vishnu had come as Lord Rama in His seventh incarnation with a view to slaying the demons Ravana and Kumbhakaran. Shiva and Sati were roaming in the forest of Dandaka. Just then Rama and His brother Lakshmana passed in front of them in search of Sita whom Ravana had abducted. Rama wore a very sad face and was almost in tears due to the loss of His beloved wife Sita. Shiva on seeing Rama instantly recognised Him as the Lord. He paid Him His respect. Sati, unaware of the identity of Rama, was taken aback to see the All-powerful Lord bowing to an ordinary mortal, and still more astonished to see that the person was being taken as the Almighty God. How could the All-mighty lose a wife, and how could He behave like a mortal, grief-stricken and lamenting as an uxorious husband! She became doubtful. And, in spite of Shiva's persuasion, She was not convinced. Finally She sought permission from Her Lord to carry out a test to be confirmed of the truth.

Sati disguised Herself as Sita and paced in front of Rama. The latter on seeing Her joined His hands respectfully and bid Her *namaskar* (salute). He then inquired the reason for Her roaming alone in the forest and the absence of Lord Shiva by Her side. Sati got upset and almost lost all consciousness. She sat down on the wayside. On recovering, She opened Her eyes and looked around. Wherever She looked at, Her eyes met Lord Rama, Sita and Lakshmana walking together. She was now convinced of the Almighty's glory and returned to Shiva. Ashamed of Herself she lied to Shiva of having carried out any test. Shiva felt having been betrayed and forsook Her.

Sati was now living a lonely and miserable life with dreary days and weary nights. Shiva was indifferent to her and soon got into a trance. Sometime later Sati's father, Daksha, was holding a *yajna* (sacrificial fire). She came to know about it and begged permission from Her Lord to attend it. Shiva warned Her that She was not invited, and it would not do any good to Her to attend it uninvited. However, Sati trusting that She needed no invitation to go to Her own father, persuaded Her Lord. Finally Shiva, left with no alternative, gave Her the free will.

Sati's Sacrifice

When Sati called at Her father's house, She was given a very cold reception. Except for Her mother, nobody cared about Her. Furthermore She did not see any arrangement made for the accommodation of any of these Lords - Brahma, Vishnu and Mahesh in the *yajna*. She then recalled the warning given by Shiva. She flew into a temper and threw Herself into the *yajna*. Before dying She begged for forgiveness from Her Lord, took His image into Her heart and made a prayer to be His wife in the next birth. When Shiva learnt about the happening He came with His retenue and destroyed everything. Daksha pleaded for mercy, and was saved. He repented for all his misdoings and soon became one of the staunchest devotees of Shiva

Parvati's birth

Later Sati took birth as Uma in the house of Himachal, the deity presiding over the mountains. Taking birth and living within hail of the mountains, She was also called Parvati (*parvat* meaning mountain). Right from Her childhood She underwent penances and performed untold sacrifices to have Shiva as Her Lord. At the request of all the gods and in particular of Rama, Shiva broke His trance, and accepted to wed Parvati.

Celebrating the festival

This festival is celebrated mostly by women and young unmarried girls. The married women worship Parvati in order that their conjugal life lasts long and happy. Spinsters pray to have a

*Shivaayai hara kaantaayai
Prakrityai srishti hétawé
Namastee brahma chaarinyai
Jagaddhaatryai namo namah.*

handsome bridegroom with all sterling qualities. Devotees wake up early, and after taking a bath they clean their *puja* room and

Mother Parvati

the idols. Mother Parvati and Shiva are garlanded, and offered *prasad*, fruits and flowers. Recitations from the *Shiva Puranas* are done, and prayers in praise of the couple are sung.

One would remember that Mother Sita had called at the shrine of Parvati before her wedding. She had prayed to Her with joined hands -

> *"Glory, all glory to you, O daughter of the mountain King! Glory to you, who gaze on the countenance of the great Lord Shiva as a Chakora bird on the moon. Of all good women who adore their husband as a god, Mother you. rank foremost. All who adore your lotus-feet, Shining One, attain happiness, be they gods, men or sages. You know my heart's longing since you ever dwell in the town of every heart. That is why I have refrained from openly declaring it."*

Mother Parvati was highly pleased. Alive and outgoing in Her love and sympathy for Her devotees She responded most favourably. The wreath from Her neck dropped on Sita's. She smiled to Her and blessed Her -

> *"Hear, Sita, my infallible blessing. Your heart's desire shall be accomplished. Narada's words are ever faultless and true; the suitor on whom your heart is set shall indeed be yours."*

Teej

A festival which is closely related with Mother Parvati is the *Teej*. It is celebrated in the month of *Asadha* (June/July). A lively celebration, it is held solely by women and young girls. The festival takes place in several parts of India, but is more popular in Rajasthan. Swings are hung from trees and in houses, and women in their colourful attire sing in praise of Mother Parvati. The devotees first worship the Mother in their houses. They then take the images of the deity and accompanied by music and devotional songs.go in procession throughout the main streets of the cities. In Jaipur the procession is accompanied by a retenue of elephants and camels.

Ganga Dussehra

The *Ganga Dussehra* festival is celebrated on the *dashmi* (tenth day) in the bright fortnight *(suklapaksh)* of the month of *Jyeshtha* (May/June). On this day the sacred river Ganga had descended to the earth for the welfare of mankind. She is considered as the elder sister of Parvati, daughter of Himavan and Mena, and had her abode in the heavens. She was brought down to earth through great penances performed by Bhagirath, great grandson of King Sagara to redeem the soul of the 60 000 sons of the king. People in India go to the sacred river Ganga to have a ritual bath, and places like Rishikesh, Hardwar, and Benaras are always crowded on this occasion. The Sagara Island, in West Bengal, holds a very big fair on this day as it is believed that the river Ganga entered at this point in the ocean to wash away the bones of the 60,000 sons of King Sagara.

Those devotees who cannot reach Ganga go to other rivers, or purify the available water by pouring some *Gangajal* to have a bath. It is believed that by taking a bath in the Ganga and performing certain rites, one is freed form all sins, and is purified. The bath also generates an all round welfare in one's life. When people die and are cremated, the ash is taken and dipped into the Ganga to pave the soul's journey ahead. It has become a practice in Mauritius too for people to take their parents' and relatives' ashes to the Ganga when they go on pilgrimage to India.

Dusshera

The word *Dusshera* comes from the Sanskrit phrase - *Dasa bidha pap hara* which means that by performing rituals in the sacred Ganga one gets rid of sins like extortion, theft, immoral sexual activity, foul speech, backbiting and violence. However once repentance is done through the bath and the rituals, and the devotee is absolved of all sins, a vow has to be taken as not to incur such sins again. According to the *Agni Purana* and the *Padma Purana* it is said that by the thought and repetition of the name of Ganga one achieves both material benefits during lifetime on the earth and salvation after death.

Puja

Devotees have a bath in the early morning and perform their usual *puja* at home. Soon after, they take their offerings which may consist of a coconut, flowers, fruits, betel leaves and nuts, and proceed to a river bank, seaside or to the GangaTalao to perform the *puja*. They prepare what is called the *pitha* (dough) with flour and spread it on a rock. They make all the offerings to

Offerings to Mother Ganga

Mother Ganga and invoke Her blessings through *mantras* and recitations from Scriptures. They burn camphor on betel leaves and offer the light to the deity. To close the *puja* they give the *arag* which involves pouring water gently and reverentially from a *lota* (pot) down to the ground. The *pujari,* if present, helps in the ceremony which he closes by performing a *hawan*.

Gayatri Jayanti

The *Gayatri Jayanti* is held on the same day as the *Ganga Dussehra* which is on the *dashmi (tenth day)* of the month of *Jyeshtha* (May/June) Gayatri is the mother of the *Vedas,* and the festival is held to celebrate her birthday anniversary. The day is also the *Gayatri Japa* day and the *Gayatri Mantra* is -

*"Om bhur bhuvah svah tat savitur varenyam
Bhargo devasya dheemahidhiyo yo naha prachodayaat."*

नमस्ते देवी गायत्री सावित्री त्रिपपटेऽक्षरे ।
अजरे अमरे मातस्त्वाहि माम् भव सागरात् ॥

"We meditate on the glory of that Creator, who has created the universe, who is fit to be worshipped, who is the embodiment of knowledge and light, who is the remover of all sins and ignorance. May He enlighten our ignorance."

While chanting the *Gayatri mantra*, it should be broken into five parts, and a short pause should be allowed at each break -

*"Om ..... bhur bhuvah svah .....tat savitur varenyam bhargo
Devasya dheemahi .....dhiyo yo nah prachodayat."*

Each word of the *mantra* embodies the highest concept of the Absolute. It is the impregnable spiritual armour that guards and protects the one who recites it. The very meaning of *Gayatri* is *'that which protects one who sings it.".*It transforms man into the divine and endows him with the highest spiritual light. One can do the *japa mala* (reciting the *mantra* with the help of the rosary of 108 beads) a few times daily, or at least once in the morning before taking to one's daily chores and once in the evening when performing the *sandhya* (ceremonial lighting of the lamp before dusk). Whatever be the way of worshipping, or whoever be the chosen deity, the *mantra* fits in as it is a universal mantra to the Almighty Supreme Spirit. Repeating the mantra 1008 times is still better as it is the most powerful of all mantras **"Na gayatryah para mantrah--- *There is no mantra greater than the Gayatri."***

Both *mantras* and *prathnas* are chanted to God. However the *mantra* seems in some way to be different from a *prathna*. A *mantra* is meditated upon from the inner voice alone in a silent corner and repeated a number of times usually 108 or 1008 times using mostly the *jap mala* (rosary). A *prathna* is rather chanted audibly and can be done either alone or in groups. The *mantra* has a deeper appeal and usually relates to calling for spiritual power or a boon, while the *prathna* mostly sings the glory of the deity.

Legend

The legend regarding Gayatri Mata is linked with Brahma. One day Brahma was holding a sacrifice and as in all sacrifices both members of the couple had to participate. It so happened that Saraswati was away on some errand. In order to complete the sacrifice Brahma looked for a partner, and decided to wed the first woman around. He looked around and found a beautiful shepherdess. He took her for his wife and completed the ceremony. As from then Gayatri has come to be known as the second wife of Brahma. Gayatri is said to have five heads which represent the four *Vedas* and the fifth God Himself. She bears ten hands.

Namasté devi gaayatri saavitri tripadéksharé
Ajaré amaré maatas traahi maam bhavasaagaraat.

Goddess Gayatri

Nirjala Ekadashi

An *ekadashi* (eleventh day) *vrat* is held in every fortnight of each month to propitiate Lord Vishnu. As such one can see that twenty-four *ekadashis* are observed in a year. On this day devotees keep fast and undergo penance, as it is believed that spiritual influences flow toward the earth for contemplation. Keeping fast means abstaining from salty food, but one is usually allowed to take fruit, milk or a light sweetmeal However on some *ekadashis*, devotees have to keep complete fast, abstaining from taking even water - *nirjal*. The *Nirjala Ekadashi* also known as the *Bhimsen Ekadashi* is held in the bright fortnight (*suklapaksh*) of *Jyestha* (May/June). Traditionally two *ekadashis*, one in the bright fortnight of *Asadha* (June/July), and the other four months later in the bright fortnight of *Kartika* (October/November) have particular significance. They are respectively the days on which Lord Vishnu annually falls asleep (*Sayani Ekadashi*) and awakens (*Prabhodini Ekadashi*).

Nirjala Vrat

When the *nirjala ekadashi (Sayani)* is observed in the bright fortnight (*suklapaksh*) of the month of *Ashadha* (June/July) the last meal on the eve has to be taken before sunset. After performing the *sandhya* (lighting of the divine lamp before dusk), devotees spend some time reading from the *Vishnu Purana* and *Markandaya Purana*. The *vrat* can be taken by both men and women.

In the morning of the *Vrat* devotees have a bath and perform their *pujas*, worshipping in particular Lord Vishnu. Flowers, fruits, incense, holy basil leaves and *prasad* are offered, and prayers are recited. A mixture, *panchamrita*, using the five ingredients, milk, ghee, curds, honey and sugar, is prepared. It is offered to the deity, or sometimes the *saligram* (an oval stone representing Lord Vishnu) is given a bath with it. The image or idol of the deity is adorned using various articles such as new clothes and jewelry. Devotees spend the whole day fasting, reading and discoursing from the scriptures. Stories about Lord Vishnu in his various incarnations are recalled. A night of vigil is kept, again chanting praises of Lord Vishnu. The fast is broken the next morning on the *duadashi* (twelfth day) after taking some *panchamrita*.

Spiritual aspirants can expect to derive much benefit from the observance of this festival. It paves the way towards God realisation. Seekers of material gains are ensured of a prosperous and happy life.

Bhimsen Ekadashi

Once Yudhisthir, Arjun, Nakul, Sahdev, their common consort Draupadi, and their mother Kunti were keeping fast. Bhimsen, one of the brothers, was not holding the fast. He could hardly go without a meal. The mother, Kunti, had to provide him with more that half of any meal she would cook for the family. The other members of the family had to be contented with the rest. That day Sage Vyasa called on the Pandavas. He was surprised that Bhimsen was not keeping the fast. When inquired, Bhimsen explained that as a substitute for his inability to keep the fast he was making other observances such as praying, meditating and giving *daan*. Vyasa then informed him that there could never be any substitute for this fast, and that one would never reach *Vaikunth*, the abode of Vishnu, without keeping the fast. Since then Bhimsen started holding the fast which came to be known as *Bhimsen Ekadashi* as well.

Vata Savitri Vrat

The *Vat-Savitri-Vrat* is held on the *purnima* (full moon day) of *Jyestha* (May/June), but many devotees celebrate the festival for three days as from the *triodashi* (thirteenth day). The fast is kept by married women to invoke the blessings of the Lord in order that their husbands live long, happy and in plenty. The festival honours Savitri who by virtue of her chastity and devotion to her husband won his life back from Yama, God of Death. According to the *Bahmavaivarta Purana*, married women also worship the *Vata* (banyan tree) on this day as did Savitri.

Vata

After taking a bath, and wearing new clothes and ornaments, women keep fast. They go to the *vata* tree commonly known as the *bar* tree in Mauritius for worship. They apply vermillion and saffron to it. They tie a cotton thread round it and offer the *saptadhana* (seven grains) - *dhan* (rice), *gehun* (wheat), *bajra* (millet), *urad* and *moong* (lentils), *channa* (chick pea) and *jawar* (sorghum). Devotees sometimes use other grains when some of them are not available. While worshipping they go seven times round the tree. The *vata* tree is looked upon as a symbol of longevity and immortality - it hardly dies because its branches keep on striking roots and the tree keeps on spreading. After the *puja* women take their offerings home and in the evening break the fast with them.

Savitri Deified

The story originates from the *Mahabharata*. Savitri, daughter of King Aswapati, was a beautiful and virtuous princess. But in spite of all his efforts her father could not find a bridegroom correspondingly handsome and virtuous for her. One day Savitri left for the forest in company of some maids. She reached a hermitage where the blind exiled king Dyumotsena, his wife and their young and handsome son Satyavan were staying. When Savitri and Satyavan met, it was love at first sight.

Savitri on her return apprised her father of the good news. All was set for a glorious wedding when Sage Narada appeared. He informed them that Satyvan's life was short and would die just after one year of marriage. In spite of strong dissuasion by her parents Savitri stuck to her decision of wedding him, and no one else. The king had to give in to her wishes.

The couple lived happily for a year. As the fated day was approaching, Savitri watched Satyavan's steps like a shadow. One day while attempting to cut down a tree, Satyavan felt an acute pain in the head and fell unconscious to the ground. His wife took him in her lap. Yama, God of Death, sent his *dutas* (messengers) to take away the life of Satyavan. But Savitri would not let them. In spite of all their effort, they failed. Finally Yama himself came and tried hard to take the life from Satyavan's body. He could not because of her chastity and unalloyed devotion to her husband. Finally they came to an agreement. Yama would take the life of Satyavan in exchange of three irreversible boons he would grant her.

When Yama left Savitri followed him and requested for her three boons. Yama readily accepted. In the first instance she asked that her father-in-law, King Dyumatsena, should get back his eyesight. "Your wish will be honoured!", replied immediately the God of Death. "My father-in-law should get his lost kingdom back!", was the second request. "Your wish will be fulfilled!", replied unhesitatingly Yama. "May I be the mother of 100 sons!" was the third request. "Your wish will be maintained!," replied spontaneously Yama as usual without giving much thought, and left.

Thinking that all the boons had been granted, Yama left with Satyavan's life. But after some time when he turned back, he was surprised to see Savitri sobbing, and still following him. When he inquired, she replied as to how she could, as a *sati,* have 100 children without her husband. Yama could not go back on his word. He gave Satyavan back to her. The couple was united once again and lived for a very long time with a retinue of a hundred children.

Kabir Jayanti

Kabir Jayanti is the celebration of the birth anniversary of Sant Kabir. It is held on the *purnima* (full moon day) of the month of *Jyestha* . However Kabir's birth is shrouded in mystery, and his date of birth and lineage can at best be guessed from sources other than historical. References to his life have been made in the *Kabir Bani* which is to be found in *Shri Guru Granth Sahib, Kabir Bijah* and various Kabir *Granthevalis* edited by scholars. These too cannot substantiate evidence as the earliest work came out fifty years after the death of the *Sant*. Anyhow based on these sources and the works of other scholars, the accepted years about Kabir's life could be that he might have been born in the year 1455 and died in 1575. Kabir is therefore assumed to have lived for 120 years. He probably took his birth in Kasi (Varanasi) and may have died in the town of Magahar away from Kasi. As to his lineage, it is believed that he was born of Hindu parents but was found and brought up by a Muslim called Ali (popularly known as Niru). Was he a Hindu or a Muslim? This issue has remained embedded in the realm of imagination.

Kabir was married and his wife's name was Loi, but it seems that his married life had not been a happy one. He may have married a second time. From Loi he had a son Kamal, and a daughter Kamali. Many believed that the two wives as mentioned by researchers and scholars could be his own projection of *maya* (illusion) and *bhakti* (devotion). Whether he was married or not one can hardly deny the fact that he had not been a profoundly romantic man. His poems, in all splendour, sing of beloved passions.

Guru

Kabir belonged to a family of weavers, and a weaver's life was very hard both on the social and economic plane. Since his early youth he expressed great interest and delight in spiritual concern. He could have been illiterate in the sense that he might never have attended formal schooling. But Kasi, being the cradle of spiritual and religious development he must have learnt and been educated through the *guru-disciple* relationship, mostly through discourses and hearing. To Hindus his *guru* must have been Swami Ramananda. Once to attract the attention of Swami Ramananda, he lay on the steps of the *ghat* at the sacred river Ganga where the *Swami* used to come to take the ritual dip in the very early hours of the morning. The *Swami* stepped on his body in the dark, and to apologise for the act he muttered the holy name of Rama. Kabir took this name as a *mantra* and as an invitation for his spiritual initiation. Others believe that a *suri* sage Sheikh Taro and Pitambar Pir must have been his teachers. Be it what it may Kabir had always profound respect and devotion for his *gurus*. Of Ramananda he said:-

> "On meeting Guru Ramananda
> O Kabir
> All my ambivalence
> And suffering
> Are vanished
> For ever! "

The *guru* had removed the veil of illusion from his eyes. He had come like a thunderous cloud of rain which helped him to blossom into a flower, a flower that has ever been bristling with love, joy and justice.

Moksha

It is believed that Kabir had achieved *moksha* (liberation) at the age of twenty-three. His eloquence and rendering of love and truth had been so striking that it disturbed the well-entrenched religious establishment of his time. It hurt the feelings of the *pandits* and *maulas* in Kasi. He was brought to the court of the then ruling Muslim administrator. He was jailed and even sentenced to death. Legends have it that he miraculously escaped the three death sentences passed against him, namely -

1. by being thrown into the river Ganga, hands and feet bound
2. by being thrown into blazing fire, and
3. by being trampled by a wild elephant.

Finally he was sent in exile away from Kasi, as any punishment inflicted upon him was matched with a still deeper sense of conviction for his irreversible truth and eloquence.

His death

Kabir stood for world brotherhood and more particularly for Hindu-Muslim unity. He refrained from asserting that he himself belonged to either of the two. He had never been a professional ascetic. He sang of love and love only for his 'Beloved' :-

> *"With Thy Light,*
> *O My Beloved*
> *Come into*
> *My Eyes!*
> *Shall Adore You*
> *For ever"*

Kabir has left an indelible imprint and has conquered the hearts of all. For socially concerned suffering millions he had been a revolutionary who sang against the tyranny of the powerful, for spiritual seekers he had been a great *yogi*, for men of letters he had been a poet *par excellence*, to the oppressed *a mahatma*, to the lovers a man of romance, and to humanity at large an *avatar*. He belonged to humanity, far far away from the realms of caste, creed and status. At his death both Hindus and Muslims wanted to perform the last rites according to their customs. The Hindus willing to cremate him while the Muslims to bury him. His body was kept in a room and covered with a cloth. At the time they wanted to perform the rites, they removed the shroud, and what they saw was a bouquet. Be it legend or otherwise, the meaning is crystal clear. It spelt the fragrance of romance, mystery of divine presence and symbol of eternal love.

Guru Purnima

> *"......the pupil as a tender climber, and the teacher, the supporting tree round which the climber twists and turns in quest for the light of knowledge"* (Dayendranath Burrenchobay)

Indeed the *guru* is the guiding light that saves the disciple from falling into the abyss of ignorance. And the *Guru Purnima* is the day when the disciple is called upon to pay his deep debt of gratitude owed to his *guru*. The festival is held on the *purnima* (full moon day) in the month of *Ashadha* (June/July). It is the birthday of the great sage Maharishi Vyasa who has edited the four *Vedas*, written the eighteen *Puranas,* and the *Mahabharata* which contains the memorable *Bhagavad Gita*. A most fitting tribute is paid to him before embarking on the study of his works

> *"Salutations unto thee, O Vyasa of broad intellect and with eyes large like the petals of full blown lotuses, by whom the lamp of knowledge, filled with the oil of the Mahabharata has been lighted."*

"Namastute Vyaasa vishaala buddhe phullaaravindaayatapatra netra Yena twayaa Bhaarata tailapoornaha prajvalitogyaana maya pradeepah."

All spiritual aspirants and devotees perform the Vyasa *puja* on this day in remembrance of their *gurus.* The *gurus* have imparted knowledge and wisdom, and spread light in and around them. Indeed the very meaning of the word *guru* is one who removes darkness (*gu* - darkness, *ru* - remover). On this day the disciples express their gratitude to the *gurus* and offer them *daan* such as flowers, fruit, new clothing and *dakshina* (gifts). For the devotee whose *guru* is dead he performs the *tarpan*. He performs the *puja* on a white flower which is invoked as his *guru*. He is worshiped through offerings like flowers and fruits accompanied by *mantras*.

To attain God realisation which should be the goal of man, one needs the *guru* to acquire knowledge. And together with the *guru* one also needs the scriptures. These are the two eyes which restrict the mind. The scriptures are like the maps and charts that guide a traveller on his way. But to read and interprete correctly the maps and the charts one needs knowledge and skill which can be given only by the *guru*, because he has verified them in his own practice and reached the goal. However much a disciple can claim to be versed, he still has to resort to the *guru* if not to learn from him but at least to verify the validity of his experience and the soundness of his knowledge.

The Guru as God

Our scriptures have deified the personality of the *guru,* and to adore the *guru* is indeed to adore the Supreme Being -

*"Gurur Brambha, Gurur Vishnu, Gurur Devo Maheshwarah,
Gurur Shakshat Param Brambha Tasmai Shri Guruve Namah".*

The *guru* is the representative of the Almighty on earth. He is like the ambassador who is sent to a foreign country to represent his own. The host country hails him with all due honour, and sees in him the voice and dignity of the country he represents. His seat and himself become a mark of respect. Likewise, the *guru* who holds the same position as the representative of the Almighty, should be given all due honour and be worshipped as God Himself. Another comparison could be the honour and respect given to a flag. It is but a piece of cloth, yet the honour and dignity invested in it make of it a mark of highest distinction.

Vyasa versus Ganesha

It is said that Ganesha has been the scribe of the epic *Mahabharata* while Vyasa dictated it. Conditions were set by each other when they embarked on their task as narrator and scriber. When Vyasa assigned the task to Ganesha, the challenge was that the former should not break the flow of his speech. Vyasa reacted by stating that Ganesha should understand each and every word of the text that he would be writing. He should not waive his pen even for an instant. When the work began, Vyasa however occasionally wanted to have some rest and made the verses very difficult to compel Ganesha to stop and think. It is argued that Ganesha never gave Vyasa the chance to rest, and wrote uninterruptedly. At some time while writing, his pen became blunt and broke down. He instantly took one of his tusks and repaired to his job. This may explain the single tusk (*ekadanta*) that Ganesha has.

चैतन्यं शाश्वत शान्त व्योमातीतनिरंजनम् ।
नाद बिन्दु कलातीत तस्मै श्री गुरुवे नमः ॥

*Chaitanyam shaashwatam shaantam
Vyomaateetam niranjanam
Naada vindu kalaateetam
Tasmai shree guruvé namah.*

Naag Panchami

Naag Panchami is celebrated on the *panchami* (fifth day) of the bright fortnight (*suklapaksh*) of the month of *Shravana* (July/August). It is a festival observed in honour of snakes which are held in reverence by devotees. Lord Shiva wears a snake round His neck - *"bhujagendrahanam"*. The snake symbolises the basic dormant energy which in cobra-like style is coiled at the bottom of the spinal cord. It is known as *kundalini shakti*, the serpent force. Lord Vishnu rests on His couch, the *Shesh Naga*

Lord Vishnu on His couch, the Shesh Naga

in the milk-ocean. His seat is described as *"bujagendrasayanam."* Lakshmana, the brother of Lord Rama, in the epic *Ramayana* is considered to be the *avatar* of the *Shesh Naga*. The *Shesh Naga* holds the earth on his head.

Puja

On this day devotees after taking a bath and performing their usual *puja*, keep fast. According to the *Garur Purana* devotees make *murthis* (idols) of snakes on both sides of the house. Some devotees draw the images of snakes on the walls of their houses. And those already having the images which could be of stone, metal or wood would have them washed and cleaned.

They then perform the usual welcoming rituals, and offer flowers, fruits and milk to the *Shesh Naga*

Since this festival takes place in *Shravana*, which is a rainy season in India, it is not uncommon to see snakes as they have to come out to look for food and shelter. To protect themselves, people resort to prayers and worship them for their mercy. They offer them milk and sweetmeal, and recite prayers. The snakes after taking the meal usually go away.

In some parts of India, trappers are engaged to get snakes and bring them to the *shivalas* or other places of worship. Charmers are also called to partake and help in the rituals. At the end of the *puja* they are set free or taken back to the forests. At times when snakes are not available, devotees make cloth effigies of mythical serpents, or go to images carved in stone, clay or metal. Artists may be called upon to draw and paint snakes on paper, cloth or board. They are reverentially displayed and worshipped.

In Mauritius

Some people hold the view that this festival was widely held in bygone days in Mauritius, when it was believed that snakes did come out and visited the devotees. They prepared the *lawa* (roasted *dhan*), and kept it together with some milk in a corner of their yard in the evening. They were pleasantly surprised the next morning to notice that the food had disappeared, and were convinced that it had been eaten by some snake. This could be true to some extent, as long ago Mauritius was almost covered with tall grass and woodland. However the existence of harmful snakes could be disputed, it would rather refer to adders, harmless little snakes which are hardly to be found in residential quarters today.

Legend

Once the seven sons and daughters-in-law of a brahmin family were living together. On a *Naag Panchami* day the elder six daughters went to visit their brothers. The youngest, having no brother, stayed at home and prayed the *Shesh Naga devta* taking him as her brother. As soon as the *puja* was completed, the *Shesh Naga* disguised as a poor brahmin appeared, and invited her to his place. She accepted, and on the way the brahmin revealed his identity. The daughter-in-law was very happy and still happier when she was invited to stay for some time in his abode. During her stay she was offered two silver lamps as a present. While she was attempting to light them, one lamp fell on the infants of the deity and hurt them seriously. The deity's wife was so angry that in addition to expelling her made up her mind to wreak vengeance on her at some appropriate time.

The deity's wife chose the following *Naag Panchami* day to visit her and avenge herself. On calling at her abode she was surprised to see that the daughter-in-law, in spite of the insult inflicted upon her, was continuing to keep her fast and performing the rituals with unabated faith. She was moved by her faith and devotion, and consequently befriended her. The *Naga* family was so happy, that the *Shesh Naga* declared that anybody praying him on that day would be considered his brother.

Tulsidas Jayanti

Tulsidas Jayanti is the birthday anniversary of the poet Tulsidas, and is held on the *asthami* (eighth day) of the bright fortnight (*suklapaksh*) of the month of *Shravana* (July/August).

His Birth

The poet is believed to have been born in the year 1503 and to have died in 1623 at the age of 120 years - a span of life usually attributed to a sinless man. However some scholars dispute the year of his birth, arguing that he might have been born in 1532, thus shortening his life period to only 91 years. He was born in a poor Brahmin family, his parents did not welcome his birth believing that he was born under the spell of an unfavourable star.

However to his devotees the story is quite different and enshrouded in mystery. He is said to have been born as a child of five with all his teeth in his mouth. The first sound that came from him was Ram, and hence he was named Rambola. His mother died almost immediately after his birth, and his father, Atmaram Doobay did not survive his wife much longer. He was born under the *mool nakshtra* considered very inauspicious. He was taken care by Narhari, a *pujari* (priest) who imparted to him the basic education and religious observances. Because of his fondness for rituals and learning and his particular devotion to the *tulsi* (holy basil) plant, he was given the name of Tulsidas. Every morning and evening he would pray and water the plant.

A legend would have that when the boy Tulsidas became an orphan, Mother Parvati took the place of the mother lost to him in the early childhood, and attended to all his needs. She was sent by Lord Shiva who knew that Tulsidas had taken birth to write and glorify Rama's incarnation. To Shiva Rama was his *Istadeva*.

Ratnavali

When Tulsidas grew up he married a young and lovely maiden, Ratnavati. As all newly married couple, they were spending the days quite happily. And as the days went by Tulsidas grew fonder and fonder of his wife, to the extent that he could hardly part company with her. He would often neglect his work to be by her side.

Ratnavati was once invited by her parents to spend a few days at their house. Tulsidas could not accompany her as he was entrusted with some urgent responsibility by his *guru*. On his return home Tulsidas could not adapt himself to the lonely situation. And soon the pang of separation became unbearable.

Tulsidas left the house to proceed to his father-in-law's residence. It was the rainy season. The night was stormy. Thunder roared and lightning flashed. The rivers were flooded. Not a soul on the way. Unmindful of the dangers and inconveniences of the situation Tulsidas made himself bold and started on his journey. After a hard struggle against the inclemencies of the weather he finally reached his father-in-law's house. The doors and windows were closed and Ratnavati was sleeping on the upper floor. Tulsidas could not find any means to climb up and get into the house. Through a flash of lightning he saw something which he took for a rope. Holding it he climbed up and knocked at the door. Ratnavati was surprised to see Tulsidas at this late hour of the night in such a stormy weather and beside him a snake which she immediately identified as being a rope used by her husband. Hearing the noise Ratnavati's parents came up.

Ratnavati felt ashamed at her husband's doing and his blind passion. She flew into a wild temper and started scolding him. She rebuked him harshly as she could not understand how he could be so blind to sensual pleasure -

Hadh chaam ke deha mamah tapar eissi prithi

Tason adhi jo hota ram par mit jati bhawa bheeti"

> **"This body is made of five tatwa (elements) - agni (fire), vayu (wind), jal (water), prithvi (earth) and akash (ether). It will soon decay! What is its worth and that you are so fond of! If you had given yourself to God - to His love and devotion - you would have since long attained moksha (final beatitude)!**

He was stunned to hear the stingy remark made by his wife. He sat for a while, pondered over it and soon left the house.

In search of God

Tulsidas now beside himself could see through his weakness. How true the words of his beloved wife! He soon embarked on his endless voyage in search of the Lord. Where to find the Lord? He wandered from forest to forest, over vales and hills, and looked for hermits, sages and saints to guide him. He called on sacred river banks, climbed up mountain tops, and crawled in caves, hoping to find someone to direct him to the Lord. In spite of all his efforts his attempt was unsuccessful.

Finally being tired of roaming about endlessly he sought shelter under a tree. During the night a voice from the tree woke him up. He asked him to do him a favour by bringing some water to him, and that in return he would be able to help him in his goal. That was the ethereal body of a man who had not been able to get salvation after his death and has had to find abode in that tree. Tulsidas helped him by providing some water to quench his thirst. In return the ethereal body gave him the clue that only Hanuman could open the gateway to the Lord.

How and where to find Hanuman ! The ghost informed him that a *Ram katha* was being held in a nearby *shivala* every night, and he used to be present there unfailingly. Clad in ragged clothes he was the first to come and the last to leave the place. Tulsidas called at the *mandir* and observed. After a few days he was able to spot Hanuman. He clasped his feet and begged him to show the way to the Lord. Hanuman did all possible not to disclose his identity, but seeing the faith and devotion of Tulsidas he had to change his mind.

Lord Rama

Hanuman asked Tulsidas to come to Chitrakoot where he would be able to see Lord Rama and his brother. Hanuman climbed up a tree and Tulsidas sat down under the very tree making sandal paste in the hope to see and welcome the Lord. He was so absorbed in the preparation of his *tilak* (paste) that he was hardly aware of his surroundings. After some time the Lord and his brother, Lakshman came and requested Tulsidas to apply the paste to the forehead. He had delved so deep in his thought and expectation that he was hardly aware that the Lord was in front of him. Seeing that the Lord did not reveal Himself, Hanuman tried to draw Tulsidas's attention to His presence but he was so merged in his love and *bhakti* that he took no notice -

*"Chitrakoot ki ghat mein bhayi santan ki bhir
Tulsidas chandan ghise tilak deta Raghubir."*

The Lord while leaving blessed Tulsidas, and he was enlightened. He was all unconsciously given the meritorious boon of chanting the Lord's glory. Some say that he recognised the Lord. He took hold of His feet and would not allow Him to leave. It was only on the promise that the Lord would never forsake him that he let Him go. He went on the bank of the sacred Ganga and started writing the *Ramayana* It was the ninth day (*navmi*) of the bright fortnight (*suklapaksh*) of the month of *Chaitra* (March/April) in the *Samvat* year 1631 (Gregorian year 1574) when the first verse flowed from his pen. This day is the very birthday of His Lord. He worked untiringly and ceaselessly, and the work is said to be completed in two years seven months and twenty six days.

The Ramayana (Sri Ramacharitamanasa)

Tulsidas's birthday is celebrated with great reverence and fervour. He gave to the world the *Ramayana* whose every word absolves man from numberless sins as stated here -

*"Ramayan maha kavya, sookon vistaram
Ek ek aksharam punsam punsam, papak nasanam."*

The story of Rama has been made within the reach and understanding of the common man. Erstwhile it was in Sanskrit, and the privilege of the learned few. He wrote the epic in the *Vraj* (or *Braj*), a dialect of Hindi. He matched the grandeur and majesty of Sanskrit with the lyrical grace and power of *Vraj*, producing a language of the heart. He has imbued every verse with love and devotion to the Lord, which generates trust, strength and hope to the reader in his moment of despair. He never claimed to be a great or refined poet, on the contrary he called himself a *prakrivit Kavi* (uncultivated poet) and his language was *gramya*, that of the village folk. His greatness lies in bringing the philosophical teachings enshrined in high culture to the doorstep of the uneducated and the humble, and in having the great *pandits* of the day accept his devotional style.

In addition to the epic *Ramayana*, and *Kavitavali*, Tulsidas has produced ten other works among which the *Vinay-Patrika*, Da-

havali and *Gitavali*. However it is the matchless grandeur and devotional style of the *Ramayana* that has rocketed Tulsidas to fame. He has won the heart of the teeming millions through his

Lord Rama and Mother Sita

devotion to the Lord who was as much in his poetry as in his daily life. And whenever man is overtaken by grief and sorrow he turns to him, as in most unequivocal terms he stresses that the only salvation is God's name - *Rama! Rama! Rama!* Rama and *Ramayana* have come to stay, for ever and ever, as the beacon of hope in the face of any social and cultural decay, and along with them the name of Tulsidas.

Raksha Bandhan

The *Raksha Bandhan* festival is held on the *purnima* (full moon day) of the month of *Shravana* (July/August). It is commonly known as the *Rakhi* festival. On this day the sister full of joy and hope, and in her best attire calls on her brother. The sister first does an *aarti,* that is lighting a lamp on a decorated plate and

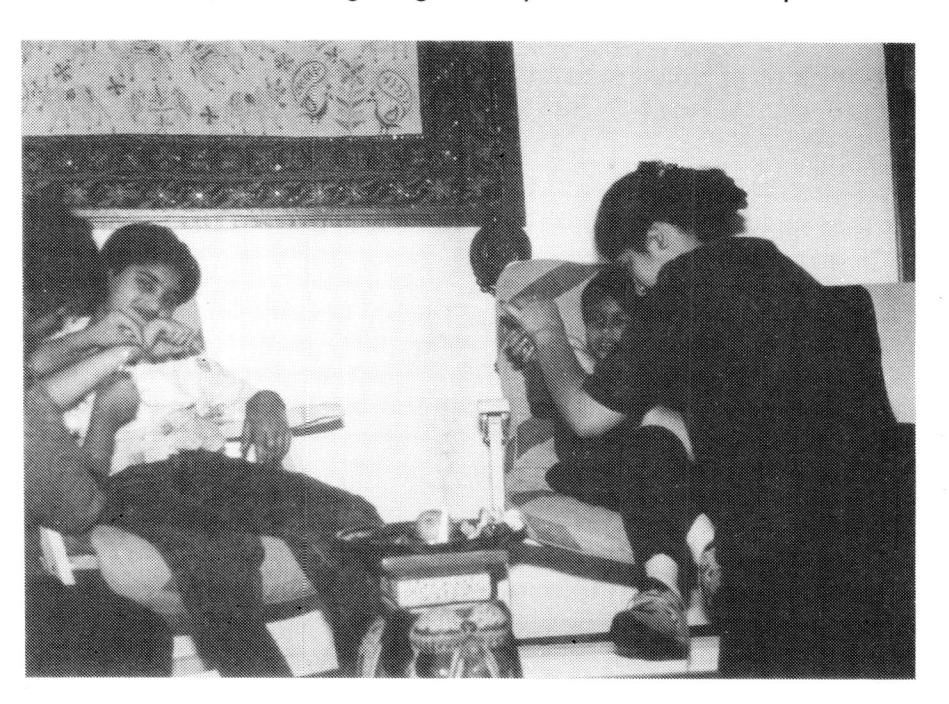

Tying the rakhi

waving it circularly in front of her brother's face. She applies the *tika* on his forefront and ties the *rakhi* (silken thread) on the right wrist of her brother. She wishes him luck, success, long and prosperous life - all that one needs to fulfill himself. The *mantra* which is recited while the *rakhi* is being tied on the wrist to import divine power to it is -

" Yena baddho balee raajaa daanavendro mahaabalah;
Tena twaan pratibadhnaami rakshey maa chala maa chala"

The sister then feeds her brother with some sweets which she takes along with her - sweets so that he is in and surrounded by sweetness throughout his life. In return the brother offers the sister a gift, a symbolic gesture of his having been very pleased.

He also pledges on this day to protect the sister, and do all within his power to keep her happy. It should be noted that a girl would call on anybody whom she considers as a brother, irrespective of class, creed and colour.

Legend

The festival does not seem to stem from a religious and still less from an agrarian concept. It rather takes its source from historical events occurring in India. However, with the passing of time the basic concept of all auspicious celebrations has been tinged with a spirit of holiness and most festivals are held against the background of religious fervour, and the *Rakhi* is no exception.

A famous story about the festival is inked with Queen Karmavati. Once Bahadur Shah was busy capturing the fortress of Queen Karmavat. In her helplessness she called for help from Emperor Humayun by sending him a *rakhi*. The latter who was far away responded to the call and hurried to save her and the fortress. Unfortunately he turned up a bit too late, and the fortress had already collapsed and the queen dead.

Another legend is the one linked with the invasion of Punjab by the mighty Alexander. It was evident that Porus, King of Punjab would not be able to stand against him. Porus's wife called secretly on Alexander and tied the *rakhi* on his wrist. It was the full moon day of *Shravana*. Alexander accepted her as his sister and being familiar with the tradition gave her the promise of help and protection. As token she begged for the life of her husband. Though Porus was defeated in the battle that took place Alexander spared his life.

Once Indra was overpowered by the demons and his city of Amaravati was on the brink of capture. His wife Sachi tied a holy *rakhi* around his wrist. The *rakhi* as a protective power helped Indra, and in the days that followed he was able to defeat the demons and retain his kingdom.

Rakhi

The *rakhi* is extensively used in the Hindu religion. The husband

and the wife tie it on each other's wrist at the performance of any ritual. Anybody before starting a *puja* would have it tied by the priest to his wrist. On the *rakhi* day brahmins and all those wearing *janeo* (sacred threads) have old ones removed and replaced by new ones. Indeed many strongly favour the argument that *Raksha Bandhan* is primarily a festival for *gurus*, *rishis* and *munis*. On this day devotees also offer libations of water to the ancient *rishis* and spend some time studying the *Vedas*. The *rakhi* is considered as a protective armour

This festival also known as the *Upakarma* is in particular sacred to those who have been invested with the sacred thread (*janeo*). The investiture opens their eye of wisdom, the third eye, and imbues them with glorious spiritual significance.

In Vedic times the *Bhaiya Duja*, somewhat similar to the *Raksha Bandhan* and known as the *Bharti Dvitiya* used to be held by sisters. They applied the *tika* on the forehead and did the *aarti* and prayed to the Almighty for their brothers' welfare. The ceremony was extended to all men going to war. Mothers, wives and sisters applied the *tika* to all the soldiers so that they would come back victorious.

Kanu Pongal

A festival reminiscent of the *Raksha Bandhan* is the *Kanu Pongal* celebrated in South India by sisters for the welfare of their brothers. It is held on the same day as the *Mattu Pongal*. Sisters perform rituals using the leftovers of sweet and salty *pongal*, betel leaves and nuts, *haldi* (turmeric) and coloured rice. They apply a *tilak* to the forehead of the brothers and wish them success, prosperity and long life. The brothers respond by giving some presents such as fruits and sweets.

Krishna Janmasthami

On the *asthami* (eighth day) in the dark fortnight (*krishnapaksh*) of the month of *Bhadrapad* (August/September) the festival of *Krishna Janmasthami* is celebrated. It is the birth anniversary of Lord Krishna who incarnated with the objectives of destroying the wicked demon Kansa, establishing righteousness and showing mankind the divine path to God - realisation.

वसुदेव सुतं देवं कंस चाणुर मर्दनम् ।
देवकी परमानन्दं कृष्ण वन्दे जगद् गुरुम् ॥

His birth

The demon king, Kansa had usurped the throne by imprisoning his own father. He was wicked and ruthless, and right from his youth he oppressed his subjects. His tyranny knew no bounds, and soon every being was overwhelmed with pain and misery. Goddess Earth and all gods led by Brahma called on Lord Vishnu, and complained of their sufferings. The Lord promised that He would incarnate as Krishna to kill Kansa, and to relieve the world from his despotic rule.

Incarnations usually come with their particular groups. For example Lord Rama came with Sita, Bharata, Lakshmana and Shatrughna. Krishna too had to have His favourite companions, Balram and Radha. Hence when Lord Vishnu decided to take birth in Mathura as Devaki's son, He arranged with *Shesh Naga* to come down earlier to earth as His brother Balram. He also requested the *Maha Maya* to be conceived in Yashoda's womb and to take birth as a child in the house of Nand and Yashoda in Gokula at the same time as His own.

Vasudeva had married Kansa's sister Devaki. Just after the wedding the sage Narada informed Kansa that Devaki's eighth son would be a threat to his life. He instantly wanted to murder the couple, but Vasudeva pleaded for mercy. He promised to deliver all infants born of Devaki to Kansa who could dispose of them as he wished. Vasudeva agreed to the condition.

Meanwhile Devaki gave birth to six children who were all handed over to Kamsa. The latter dashed them to death on a big rock outside the prison. Soon Devaki was pregnant for the seventh child. The gods went on prayer and so did the couple. By divine force the embryo was transferred from Devaki's womb to that of Rohini, another wife of Vasudeva. Kansa was told that Devaki had miscarried. When the child was born to Rohini he was called Balram. The despotic king though trusting that Devaki had miscarried nevertheless became doubtful and separated the couple. Some time after Vasudev felt a stong light and a divine heat throughout his body. The light and the heat combined into a powerful beam and moved from his body to that of his wife. The Lord thus allowed Himself to be conceived in Devaki as the eighth child.

Vashudeva sutam devam
Kansa chaanoor mardanam.
Devakee paramaanandam
Krishnam vandé jagad gurum.

The days rolled on. Soon Devaki one midnight seemingly gave birth to a child who immediately assumed the divine form of the Lord standing in front of them. His transcendental effulgence illuminated everything in all directions. His lotus-like eyes, His four arms wielding uplifted weapons - a conch, a mace, a lotus and a discus, His bosom impregnated with the mark of *Srivatsa*, His yellow garment all struck the mother with wonder. He was a *Purna Avatar* born with all the sixteen *kalas* (powers). He reminded the couple of their past life and the boon He had conferred on them. He then immediately assumed the body of a baby at the supplication of the mother.

Miraculously all the guards of the prison fell in a deep slumber and were deprived of all their cognitive faculties .The fetters loosened. The gates opened. Vasudeva and Devaki decided to have the child taken to Nand and Yashoda in Gokula. Taking Him into a winnowing basket and placing it on his head Vasudeva left for Gokula. He had to cross the river Yamuna. The night was sounding with the crack of thunder and flashing with lightning. The river was in spate. But as soon as Vasudeva stepped out all subsided to a level to allow safe and pleasant passage. The clouds reduced their intensity and rained with a gentle rumbling, the lightning softened to a guiding light, the waves receded to offer their warmth and hospitality, and the *Shesha Naga* spread itself like an umbrella over the child's head to protect Him.

On reaching his friend Nanda's house, Vasudev left the child with him. In exchange he took their new-born daughter *Maha Maya*. As soon as he returned to the cell, the doors closed by themselves, the fetters locked by themselves and the guards awoke. The girl then gave a big cry. Kansa was informed of her birth. He rushed to Devaki, snatched the child and hurried as usual to have her dashed against the stone slab. The child slipped out of his hands and while flying away informed him that his destroyer had already taken birth, and was in Gokula. Kansa was stunned. He decided to slay all the new born children in both Mathura and Gokula. However Balram, Krishna and many others never came within his reach.

A slight variation to this legend in the *Vishnu Purana* is that Vishnu took two of His hairs, one black and the other white to have Devaki impregnated. Shortly after, the foetuses were transfered to Rohini's womb by divine force. Two children were born, the fair complexioned Balram and the dark hued Krishna.

Makhan Chor

Krishna as a child was very fond of *makhan* (home-made butter), cream, curd and other milk products. He would creep into the house, climb up the shoulders of His friends to reach the high-hung pots and devour the contents. This practice was extended to the neighbours' and friends' houses. Yashoda soon got fed up with complaints from one and all. Once on receiving such a complaint she called and questioned Him. On Krishna's denial of the accusation she asked Him to open the mouth to confirm herself of the veracity of the complaint. Krishna opened wide His mouth. Great was Yashoda's astonishment when she saw the whole universe in that mouth, and she almost fainted. The Lord every now and then confirms of His presence and of His *avatar* to His devotees, and that was the opportunity for Him to do so. Once again He gave the same picture to Arjuna when the latter was at a loss before the war took place on the battlefield of Kurukshetra between the Pandavas and the Kauravas.

His flute

Krishna grew up in Gokula, with all aspects of ordinary human development associated with childhood, adolescence and adulthood. However when the occasion demanded He had to raise

Himself to superhuman level. Otherwise all His pastimes had been spent in playing, fighting and amorous escapades with the cowherd girls (*gopis*). His skill at flute playing has been the hallmark of His pastoral life. All animate and inanimate beings could not help to respond to the sweetness of His flute -

> *"On hearing the music of Krishna's flute, peacocks dance and other animals stand still and worship him with their glances, celestial maidens flying on their aerial cars above the earth become infatuated with him and shower him with flowers, rivers become smooth running and offer him lotuses, and in the heat of the day clouds let fall on him their cooling rain"* (A. G Mitchell)

To Radha, His bonded partner, the charm of the flute was the soul of her very self. To the *gopis* the call of His flute was irresistible. Whenever Krishna played the flute on the river bank on the full moon night, they all became restless. They left their husbands and homes to call on Him. When rebuked, they hit back by attributing the cause to the melody of His flute. They parted only on the promise of a dance with Him on that moonlit bank once again.

Lord Krishna on His flute

The *gopis* were deeply enamoured of Krishna, and He used to tease them out of love and affection for them. One day while they were bathing in the river, He stealthily took away all their clothes and climbed up a tree. In spite of repeated supplication He did not send the clothes back, but requested each one to come out instead and collect her clothes. Finally they gave in to His obstinacy. In return He promised to dance with them at the river bank on the full moon night - an event they were all fond of and always looked forward to.

The above should not be misconstrued and given a sensual twist. To Krishna nakedness symbolises truth. According to the methaphysical work, *Nyayamuktavali*, - "cows stand for the sense organs, mind is the herdsman, intellect is mind's mistress, and her garment is ignorance." To steal ignorance is to reveal truth".

Krishna's exploits

When Krishna was still an infant the demon of storm and whirlwind took Him away to have Him killed. Everybody got frightened and set out to look for Him. After a long search they saw the demon lying dead with Krishna sitting on his breast.

Once the demoness, Putna, most probably initiated by the villain Kansa, called at Yashoda's place. She took the form of a beautiful lady and started fondling the baby. Evil minded, she wanted to have Him suckle from her poisoned breasts. Krishna sucked so hard that she was left lilfeless on the floor.

Another story is about the snake, Kaaliya. The latter had poisoned the water of the river where it was residing to the extent that the vapour coming out was lethal to all living creatures. One day Krishna's friends drunk of its water and fell senseless. Krishna rushed to the spot, revived His friends and dived into the water. He put up such a strong fight with Kaaliya that it was almost beaten dead. Kaliya begged for pardon and left the river. Later it became one of Krishna's greatest devotees.

Once, the God of Rain, Indra, feeling jealous of Krishna's glory wanted to harm Him. He drove numberless dark clouds over Gokula which resulted in heavy downpours for days on end. The village was flooded to the extent that life became almost impossible. Krishna with his tiny little finger lifted up the *Govardan* mountain and spread it as an umbrella to provide shelter to the inhabitants.

One of Krishna's objectives for His incarnation was to kill Kansa. The latter had come to know about Krishna being with Nand. He invited the two brothers Balram and Krishna to visit his palace in Mathura. However his real intention was to devise a plot to have them killed. He arranged for a wrestling show in which mighty wrestlers were involved. He requested the two brothers to participate in the show, and selected two of the mightiest wrestlers, Chanura and Mushtika to oppose them. Krishna saw through the game and within seconds the two brothers defeated the mighty wrestlers. The defeat shattered Kansa's plot and he now openly ordered the killing of the two brothers through any means. In the uproarious alarm that followed Krishna jumped on the dais where Kansa was, took him by the throat and threw him lifeless on the ground.

Celebrating the festival

On this day, as for all Hindu festivals, devotees wake up early and have a bath. The *puja ghar* is cleaned. All the deities are worshipped, and as the festival is in honour of Krishna special prayers are meant for Him. Offerings like *prasad*, fruits and flowers are made. As Krishna was very fond of *makhan* (butter) devotees prepare some of it. Religious hymns are sung and passages from the *Bhagavata Purana* and *Gita* are read. A *jap mala* with the *mantra "Om Namo Bhagawate Vasudevaya "* is recited 108 times. Devotees keep a strict fast throughout the day, and it is broken only after midnight when the rituals are completed.

*Jhoulé jhoulé ho lall
jhoule kanhaya palana
Palana ho palana palana
jhoula jhoulé ho lall palana.*

In the evening devotees usually proceed to the *shivalas* or to such special places where the ceremony is held. They take along with them all their offerings. After their worship they listen to the priests who read from the *Bhagavata Purana* or the *Gita*. Various inspiring stories from Krishna's life are related. *Kirtans*, *bhajans* and devotional music accompany the discourses. At midnight an image of baby Krishna is bathed in the *panchamrita* - prepared with curd, milk, dried fruits, ghee and *tulsi* leaves. The image of Krishna is placed in a cradle affectionately decorated. Lullabies are sung, *aartis* are done, the image is garlanded and all ladies take turn to swing the cradle. After the ceremony the *panchamrita* and all offerings made to the Lord are shared among the devotees. They return home and break their fast.

This festival is held all over India though with more pomp and fervour in Mathura, the birthplace of Krishna. The tradition has been kept in all its splendour in Mauritius. Another festival connected with the birth of Krishna is *Dol Purnima* which is celebrated in India during the full moon day of *Phaguna* (February/March). A clay image of Krishna as a baby is placed in a cradle which is adorned with colours, leaves and flowers. Accompanied by music and devotional songs it is taken out in procession throughout the streets. People join in and share the *prasad* when the ceremony is over.

Hartalika Vrat

The *Hartalika Vrat* festival takes place on the *tritiya* (third day) of the bright half (*suklapaksh*) of the month of *Bhadrapad* (August/September). It is held in honour of Mother Parvati.

This festival is mostly observed by women who pray for a happy conjugal life. They request for the happiness, welfare and health of their husbands and children. After taking a bath, the women devotees go to their *puja* room. Besides their usual offerings like fruits and flowers, they take along with them the *sindoor* (vermillion). They worship Mother Parvati and Her Lord Shiva. She is garlanded, *sindoor* is applied and special *stutis* are addressed to her. They prepare the *khir*, a sweetmeal, and after offering this *prasad* to Mother Parvati, the family shares it. Sweet and tasty - this is what they beg from Mother Parvati for the family.

Legend

The *Bhavishyattara Purana* has a legend regarding Mother Parvati. She was the daughter of mountain king Parvat, and yet unmarried. The parents were wondering as to who should be Her suitor and everybody was speculating about some god. One day Sage Narad appeared with the proposal that She should marry Lord Vishnu. The idea commended itself. Himavat spontaneously requested that all arrangements be set in motion to that end. While everybody was busy making the preparations Parvati slipped away from the house with a few friends some time that night. She made a clay image of Shiva on the bank of a river and started worshipping Him. She called at the spot everyday and performed austere penance and meditation. She wasted Herself both in mind and body. She gave up food and lived only on air and dried leaves, whence She got the epithet *Aparna*. When Her parents came to know about the severe austerities they appealed to Her to give up the penance. This appeal won Her the epithet (U - Ma, meaning don't do this.) At last Lord Shiva was moved with the austerity of Her penance and appeared in front of Her. At the offer of a boon She opened up Her mind. Lord Shiva gave Her the solemn promise of marrying Her. Himavat was informed, and Parvati was made the consort of Lord Shiva. Parvati had been Sati and the consort of Shiva in Her previous birth. Before casting Her life in the *yajna* Her father Daksha was holding in his house She had implored that She should be the servant of the Lord in all Her successive births.

The festival is not restricted to married women only. Young maidens who desire a suitor of their choice do praise Her. Sita worshipped Mother Parvati when She saw Lord Rama in the garden. She had taken Him in Her heart and wanted to marry Him. Her request readily met the approval of Mother Parvati. The next day at the bow sacrifice, Rama was able to break Shiva's bow, and Sita was garlanded.

Ashunya - Shayanam

Instances abound about women keeping fast and undergoing sacrifices for the sake of the husband and the family. However one should not come conclude that women are the only agent of sacrifice. The Hindu way of life emphasises equal responsibility on both parties for a lasting and blissful conjugal life. Hence the

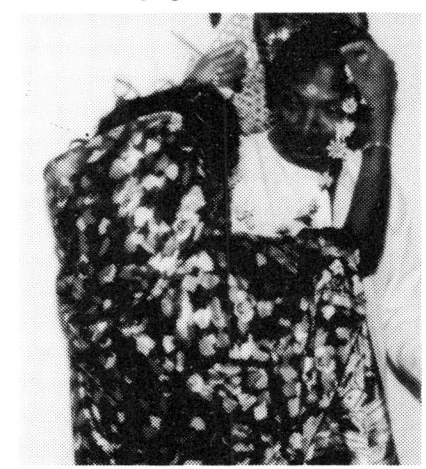

The blessed couple

celebration of the *Ashunya - Shayanam* festival. This festival is held in the month of *Shravana* (July/August), by the male partner. He pleads for the long life, health and welfare of his spouse in an ever blooming and bonded relationship with him. On this day Lord Vishnu and His consort Lakshmi are worshipped.

Ganesh Chaturthi

"I worship the lotus feet of Ganesha, the son of Uma, the destroyer of all sorrows, who is served by the host of gods and elementals, and who takes the essence of the kapittha-jambu fruit (fruit resembling the bilwa fruit)."

Gajaananam bhootaganaadisevitam Kapittha jamboophala charoobhakshanam Umaasutam shoka vinaasha kaarakam Namaami vighneshwara paada pankajam"

Ganesh Chaturthi is held on the *chaturthi* (fourth day) of the bright fortnight (*suklapaksh*) of the month of *Bhadrapad* (August/September) in honour of Lord Ganesha's birthday. He has several other names - *Vinayaka* (Remover of all Obstacles), *Ganapati* (Lord of Beings), *Gajanana* (Elephant-faced), *Gajadhipati* (God of Elephants), *Lambkhan* (Long Eared, *Lambodkar* (Pendant Belly) and *Ekadanta* (Single-Tusked). All these attributes symbolise but virtues. His pot-belly contains the whole universe, His trunk is meant to remove obstacles, His four arms usually holding a shell, a discus, a goad and a water lily represent the *Vedas*. His vehicle is a mouse which can creep through holes and cracks to achieve its goal as much as He himself symbolising an elephant can trample down everything on its path to reach the end. Thus He represents the Unity of the Small Being with the Great Being, blending the microcosm with the macrocosm, and the individual with the Supreme. He is the God of Wisdom and Success. He is invariably propitiated at the start of any ritual, or before embarking on any important project as He is the remover of all obstacles and bestower of all boons and virtues -

" *Mushakvahana modaka hastha chaamara karna vilambitha sutra vaamana rupa maheshwara putra vighna vinaayaka paada namasthe".*

Oh Lord Vinayaka! the remover of all obstacles, the son of Lord Shiva, with a form which is very short, with mouse as Thy vehicle, with sweet pudding in hand, with wide ears and long hanging trunk, I prostrate at Thy lotus-like feet'.

Adhi Devta

The *Puranas* mention that He is an *adhi devta,* that is, He had been in existence since beginningless time. For instance He is said to have been at the wedding of Shiva and Parvati, Brahma worshipped Him at the time of creation of the Universe, Vishnu prayed to Him before vanquishing Bali, Shiva propitiated Him before destroying the city of Tripura, and Mother Durga before destroying Mahishasura. Shesha Naga sought His blessing before taking up the task of supporting the Earth on his head,

Lord Ganesha

and Kamadeva, God of Love before conquering the Universe.

Ganesha's Birth

Parvati longed to have a son of Her own. The opportunity occurred when one day She was about to go for Her bath She could not see any trusted watchman at the entrance. She rubbed the dirt off Her body and made the body of a boy by mixing the dirt with oil. She then prayed to Brahma who instilled life into it. Pravati adopted the boy as Her child. She entrusted Him with the responsibility of a guard at the entrance. A strict order was given as not to allow anybody to enter the apartments. Some time later Shiva returned from the forest, and unhesitatingly tried to enter Parvati's appartment. Ganesha prevented Him from doing so. A hot worded wrangle ensued and at Ganesha's resistance, Shiva cut off His head taking Him to be an outsider. On hearing the scuffle, Parvati came to the entrance and was moved to tears at the sight of the headless boy. She lamented and pleaded with Shiva to bring the child back to life. Shiva needed a head for the child. He requested his retenue to bring Him the head of the first animal they would see. They came across a cub (child elephant) who was sleeping with her mother's back against him. They cut off his head and brought it to Shiva who placed it on the child's body to the great relief of Parvati. Ganesha was brought back to life. Following this story, it is widely believed that no mother should sleep with her back against her baby.

There is another very popular legend about Ganesha acquiring an elephant head. Ganesha was a very beautiful child with a still very lovely face. Parvati, His mother was so fond and proud of the child's face that She could not help inviting all gods to have a look at Him and bless Him. However Sani whose look was considered as being inauspicious declined the invitation. But Parvati insisted upon Sani's visiting His son. As soon as Shani glanced at Her child with his accursed look Ganesha's face got burnt. Parvati wailed, and implored to Her husband to restore the child's face. Shiva secured an elephant's head which He placed on the child's trunk. Parvati was not at all happy about the replacement, but Shiva and all gods assured Her that Ganesha would be the prime god and would be remembered first in any *puja*. He would be considered as the Lord of Beginnings.

Ganesha's Wisdom

Ganesha is worshipped first in any ritual, and one of the reasons is because of His sharpness of intellect and wisdom. Once an argument arose as to whom between Ganesha and His brother Kartikaya would be given order of preference for worship. Shiva decided that the one who would win the race round the universe would be worshipped first. Both started. While Kartikaya flew off on His peacock for the race round the universe, Ganesha went seven times in loving worship round his parents on his mouse. He then claimed that he had completed and won the race, pointing out that in keeping with the universal rule of making the *parikrama* (going round) of one's parents one has gone round the world. He was proclaimed winner in keeping with this observance. When Kartikaya came, and saw Him proclaimed victorious He got angry. He gave a blow to Ganesha and broke one of His tusks, and as for Himself He left the family to settle far away. Another reason for Ganesha having only one tusk is that Parasurama in a fight with Him cut off one of His tusks.

When Ganesha won the race everybody was happy except the moon. His wives and himself ridiculed Him when once He fell down from His vehicle in the race. Ganesha got angry and cursed the moon that on the day He would be prayed nobody would dare look at him. Hence on *Ganesh Chaturthi* day everybody would abstain from looking at the moon.

There is a variation to the legend above. Ganesha was fond of *ladoos* (sweet rice balls), and on one of His birthdays He had had too many of them. To help digest His food He went out in the open to breathe some fresh air. While He was going merrily, cheering His mouse, the serpent Vasuki crossed the path. His vehicle got frightened and stumbled. Ganesha lost His balance and fell down. His stomach burst open and the *ladoos* came out. He picked them up hurriedly, stuffed them back into His stomach and tied His belly with the serpent Vasuki. At this sight the moon and his wives burst out laughing. Ganesha got angry at this unseemly behaviour and cursed the moon saying that none would look at his face on the day His festival would be celebrated. Hence it is believed anyone looking at the moon on *Ganesh Chaturthi* day is likely to meet with bad luck. If however somebody happened to see the moon on that day he could be freed from the curse by reading or listening to the story of Lord Krishna clearing His blame regarding the theft of the *syamantaka* jewel in the *Shrimad Bhagavatam*.

Celebrating the puja

On this day devotees wake up early. They have a bath and go to the *puja* room. The room and the idols are wiped clean and shining and the usual *puja* is done. The devotees keep fast till the evening when they perform the rituals for Lord Ganesha. The *sohraso pachar pujanam* is performed with prayers and offerings like flowers, garlands, fruits, coloured powder in particular the *sindoor*. Lord Ganesha is donned with new clothes and *janeo* (sacred thread). Special offerings which are made consist of a coconut, *modak* made of gram flour and sesame seeds, twenty-one blades of *durva* grass (*chiendent*), and red flowers. However one would note that *tulsi* (basil) leaves are not offerred "*Tulashyam na ganapidam*". *Stutis* in honour of Ganesha, stories and recitations from the *Ganesha Khanda* in the *Brahma Vivartha Purana* are chanted. The *mantra* for Ganesha is "*Om

---

वक्रतुण्डे महाकाय कोटिसूर्यसमप्रभ ।
निर्विघ्नंकुरू मे देव सर्वकार्येषु सर्वदा ॥

*Vakra tunda mahaakaaya
kotisoorya samaprabha
Nirvighnam kuru mé deva
sarva kaaryeshu sarvadaa*

Shri Ganeshaya Namaha " or "*Om Gung Ganapathaye Namaha,*" and can be meditated upon 108 times through the *jap mala*. The ceremony is closed by having a *hawan* (fire worship).

In places where an icon or image is not available, devotees can use turmeric paste and shape it like a hill to represent the idol. *Avahaan* to still life in it is done, *assan* (a seat) is offered and the rituals follow as mentioned above.

This festival is celebrated with more pomp and fervour by the Marathi community in Mauritius It is celebrated over nine days. The yard and the house, in particular the *puja ghar*, is thoroughly cleaned in the preceding days. On the first day an altar is set up to accommodate the image of Ganesha usually made of clay. It is affectionately decorated so that the shrine shines in all splendour with numerous lights, colour and scent. Special rituals are performed every morning and afternoon with a variety of offerings. After their *puja* at home, devotees congregate in large numbers in daily prayer sessions at the temples or other places of worship.

At the congregation the mood is one of fulfilment and delight, as everybody is imbued with love and devotion for Lord Ganesha and convinced of His positive response. *Kirtans* and *bhajans* are sung, reading from the scriptures is done, discourses are given, and devotional music and ritual dances are performed during the whole period of observance. On the last day devotees lavishly adorn their idols. They join in groups and proceed to the nearest river or sea accompanied by religious songs and music. *Aartis* of the idols are performed all throughout the way. On reaching the sea or the river, the idols are immersed in the water with rituals, prayers and chanting. They ask for the blessing of Lord Ganesha and for His return -

"**Ganapati Bappa Morya**
Mangal Moorti Morya
Purchchya varshi laukar ya."

Father Ganapati come again,
Auspicious one come again,
Come again soon next year.

Rishi Panchami

The festival is held on the *panchami* (fifth day) in the bright fortnight (*suklapaksh*) of the month of *Bhadrapad* (August/September), on the next day of *Ganesh Chaturthi*. The *Sapta Rishis* (Seven Seers) namely Vishwamitra, Jamdagni, Bharadwaj, Gawtam, Atri, Vasistha and Kashyap who are believed to be the mind-born sons of Lord Brambha are meditated upon -

*"Kashyapotrir bharadwaajo Vishwaamitrotha gautama
Jamadagnir vasishtaashaha saptaite rishayah smritaah."*

Puja

An altar is first made. It is sanctified by applying cowdung. An eight petalled lotus is designed on the altar with coloured rice or plain flour. A copper or earthen pot filled with water and topped with a bunch of fresh mango leaves is then placed on it. The devotee performs his *puja* in front of the altar, and offers betel leaves, flowers, sundry fruits. He recites prayers with reference to the *sapta rishis*, and begs for forgiveness for any sin committed. Sometimes flowers are used to represent the *rishis*, and the rituals are performed on them. Homage is paid to them. The *tarpan*, offering of water as done during the *Pitri Paksh puja*, is carried out by some people. Devotees keep fast on this day; and except for some fruit and water they are not allowed to take anything. Along with the *rishis*, the *sati* Arundhati is also worshipped. The *puja* is usually held on the bank of a river or at the seaside. An important *mantra* recited on this day is -

"Nabyase sukla panchamyan archita rishi saptamaha dehentu papam mein sarvam grighnatwarkhia namoh namaha"

In India devotees go to the sacred river Ganga for a bath, or have a bath at home using a mixture of *Gangajal* and water from the tap. They use various objects like the soil from the holy basil plant and peepul tree, *chandan* paste, *til, awala,* and cowdung for washing their hands and performing rituals. They take 108 leaves on the head and apply water 108 times. The number 108 is considered very auspicious. The *jap mala* (rosary) has

108 beads, and whenever a *mantra* is recited it is done 108 times, and in complete faith and surrender.

Legend

One of the stories connected with Lord Shiva's son, Skanda, is related to the *Sapta Rishis*. Once the seven *rishis* were performing a *yajna* (sacrifice) where Agni was the presiding deity. In the course of the ceremony, Agni fell in love with the wives of the *rishis*. Swaha, the daughter of the *rishi* Daksha, who was already in love with Agni felt jealous when she came to know about Agni's passion for the *rishis*' wives. She disguised herself as the *rishis*' wives, and visited Agni by turn every night. She was successful in her attempts at taking the form of the wives of the first six *rishis*. However she was unable to disguise herself as Arundati, the wife of the seventh *rishi*, because of her chastity. On the sixth day (*shashti*) Swaha collected the semen of the six days out of which was born Skanda. Since Agni is another form of Shiva, Skanda is known as Shiva's own son.

Once while Swaha was returning from the nocturnal visits to Agni, she was seen by some *gandharvas* (celestial beings). The *gandharvas*, mistaking her, spread scandalous news about the *rishis*' wives. Except for Arundati all were forsaken by their husbands. However due to their innocence they were all raised to the sky as the Pleiades. When Skanda was born each of the six wives of the *rishis* claimed him to be her son. In order not to disappoint any of them Skanda developed six faces so that he could be nursed by all of them simultaneously. Thus they became his six foster-mothers.

According to another story Shiva once handed over His own semen to Agni who not being able to bear the heat deposited it in the sacred river Ganga. Its water carried the semen to a clump of reeds on one of its banks. From the semen in the reeds Skanda was born.

*Kashyapotrir bharadwaajo
Vishwaamitrotha gautamah.
Jamadagnir vasishtaashcha
Saptaité rishayah smritaah.*

कश्यपोऽत्रि भर्द्वाजो विश्वामित्रोऽथ गौतमः ।
जन्मदग्निर्वसिष्ठ च सप्तैर्त्कृपवः स्मृताः ॥

Maha Ravivar Vrat

Many devotees like to worship the Sun-God, and this takes place every Sunday (*ravivar*). In a year we therefore have about 52 *Ravivar Vrats,* out of which one is the *Maha Ravivar Vrat* (*Maha* - great, *Ravivar* - Sunday, *Vrat* - fast). It is held on the last Sunday of the bright fortnight (*suklapaksh*) of the month of *Bhadrapad* (August/September) but is subject to change in some circumstances. The Sun-God is worshipped so that the devotee is endowed with strength, intelligence, and fulfilment.

आदि देव नमस्तुभ्यं प्रसीद मम भास्कर ।
दिवाकर नमस्तुभ्यं प्रभाकर नमोऽस्तुते ॥

Aadideva namastubhyam praseeda mama bhaaskara Divaakara namastubhyam prabhaakara namostuté.

Surya is a Vedic god and has to this day been considered as an important deity. By giving light and warmth he enables all creatures to breathe with life. His influence is beyond doubt the source of all economic success. His vehicle is a chariot drawn by seven horses, or alternatively may be seem riding a horse with seven heads. His charioteer is Aruna (Red One), the elder brother of Garuda which is the vehicle of Lord Vishnu. Mention of him has been made in the Rig Veda "May Surya with its seven horses arrive" He has two wives, Samjna and Chaaya and several children among whom Yama, God of Death and Yamuna, the sacred river.

The devotee should have a bath in the river Ganga if possible, or otherwise mixes some *Gangajal* with the water at home for the purpose. After his daily usual *puja* the devotee performs particular rituals for the Sun-God. He uses red flowers for his worship, and offers red clothes, sundry fruits and *prasad*.. Of particular importance is the symbolical taking of the *panchgavya* which is a mixture of five products of the cow - milk, curd, ghee, cow urine and cowdung. The *arag* is given to the Sun in the early morning and at the close of the day before breaking the fast.

Navagrah

Planets are considered to be of great astrological significance and are likely to influence the life of an individual. Hence they have to be propitiated, and one of the ways is through the *Navagrah puja*. While performing any *yajna* or any major *puja* such as the *Shivaratri*, or *Durga puja* one has to do the *Navagrah puja*. The *Navagrah puja* (nine deities) is done by using nine short pieces of bamboo with different coloured flags. The nine deities represented are *Surya* (Sun), *Chandra* (moon), *Mangala* (Mars), *Boudh (*Mercury) *Guru* (Jupiter), *Sukra* (Venus) *Sani* (Saturn), *Rahu* (Neptune) and *Ketu* (Uranus). The last two

ब्रह्ममुरारिस्त्रिपुरान्तकारी
भानुःशशी भूमिसुतोबुधश्च ।
गुरुश्च शुक्रःशनि राहुकेतव
कुर्वन्तु सर्व मम सुप्रभातम् ॥

come from the demon Rahu who had stealthily stolen and drunk the *amrit* (ambrosia) that came out from the churning of the milk ocean (*sagarmanthan*). Lord Vishnu had cut the head of the demon Rahu, and the two pieces of his immortal body flew to the sky to move with the other planets. Along with Sani the two bodies Rahu and Ketu are considered to be very inauspicious, even malevolent.

The Navagrah deities

The coloured flags are in red for Sun and Mars, yellow for Jupiter, green for Mercury, white for Moon and Venus, and black for Sani, Rahu and Ketu. Rituals are performed in keeping with the *sorahso pachar pujanam*. The deities are given the welcome, and various offerings. The flag for the Sun as the presiding deity should be in the centre facing east, and the others around him and in specified directions. At the end of the *puja* milk and water are offered as *arag* to the Sun flag.

*Brahama muraaris-
tripuraanta kaaree
Bhaanuh shashee bhoomisuto
buddhashcha
Gurushcha shukrah
shani raahu ketawah
Kurvantu sarve
mama suprabhaatam.*

Karna

A story connected with the Sun God is the birth of Karna in the *Mahabharata*. Kunti, sister of Vasudeva, was still a child. Once the *rishi* Durvasha visited her parents, and Kunti looked after him with great care, courtesy and affection. The *rishi* was so pleased of her devotion that he conferred upon her the boon that any wish of hers would be gratified by the deity she would worship. When Durvasha left, Kunti wanted to confirm herself of the blessing given to her by the *rishi*. She invoked the deity Sun God, who resplendent in all his brilliance appeared spontaneously in front of her. Kunti was frightened by the sudden majestic appearance of the deity who instantly requested her to ask for a boon. Kunti, taken aback, murmured confusingly that she would like to have a son. The deity complied, and after some time a son was born to her through her ears. He came to be known as Karna (ears). Unmarried and still a virgin she could not account to anybody for having given birth to a child. She put the child in a basket and left him on the waters of a river.

A childless couple took Karna and brought him up as their son. When Karna grew up he joined forces with the Kauravas to fight the Pandavas - his own five brothers Yudhisthir, Bhim, Arjuna, Nakul and Sahdeo born to Kunti. In spite of his mother's persuasion to change side, he remained aloof. And in the battle between the Pandavas and Kauravas he was killed by Arjuna, through a curse given to him by a *rishi*.

Legend

A very poor and old woman used to keep the *Maha Ravivar Vrat* with much faith and devotion. On every eve of this fast she called on her neighbour to collect some cowdung to sanctify her place of worship. Once, out of wickedness, the neighbour refused to give her the cowdung. She felt very miserable, and was upset about her not being able to give the usual thorough cleaning to her worshipping corner. At night she dreamt that she was offered a cow by the Sun-God. In fact when she woke up in the morning she saw a big and lovely cow in a remote shady corner of the yard. The cow welcomed her, and since that day gave her plenty of cowdung and golden coins.

Within a few weeks the woman grew very rich. Her neighbour was surprised, and out of curiosity called on her. The old woman told her about herself and the cow. The wicked woman felt jealous and bent on harming her. She went to the king and falsely accused the old woman of having stolen the cow which she pretended was the only source of supply for her living. After the trial the cow was taken away from the old woman and given to the neighbour.

The cow now instead of giving cowdung and golden coins started filling the wicked woman's house with all sorts of filthy things. She did all within her power to stop it, and begged the cow for golden coins. But the filthy things heaped over and over until her house became an eyesore and a most unhealthy place. Soon she grew very ill and was about to die. The old and kind woman, always quick and ready in her sympathy for others, could not bear to see her miserable condition and came speedily to her. She prayed the cow and pleaded for mercy to the Sun-God. The cow responded to her prayers and the house was cleared of all its filthiness. The woman got well within a few days. She felt ashamed of her doing. She returned the cow to the old woman, and shared in the delight of the old woman's fortune.

Radha Ashtami

The *Radha Ashtami* festival is celebrated on the *asthami* (eighth day) of the dark fortnight (*krishnapaksh*) of the month of *Bhadrapad* (August/September). The day is Radha's birthday anniversary.

Radha and Krishna

Radha was the favourite companion of Krishna in Brindavan where He used to spend most of His time doing His *raas lilas* (pastimes) among the *gopis* (cowherd girls). His flute enchanted beast and man alike and made them restless, in particular Radha who hearing the wishful music of Krishna and His flute-could never hold her steps -

*"O! Krishna, I am coming,
I can no more delay,
My heart has flown to join thee,
How shall my footsteps stay!"*
(Laurence Binyon)

Radha was an *ans* (part) of Krishna, considered to have originated from Him, according to the *Vayevasvat Purana*. She could not stay without Him. She was in passionate love with Him, love not construed with passion, but love that expressed itself in selflessness, grace and devotion. Sarojini Naidu, the Nightingale of India, so beautifully translates Radha's love and anguish for Krishna -

*"My foolish love went seeking Thee at dawn
Crying O Wing, where is Kanhaya gone?*

*At dusk I pleaded with the dove-grey tides
O, tell me where my flute-player abides."*

And to Radha's moaning Krishna's reply -

"Why seekest thou My loveliness without

*And askest wind or wave or flowering dell
The secret thy within thyself doth swell?*

I am of thee as thou of me a part.
Look for me in the mirror of thy heart."

Once Rukmini and the *gopis* asked Krishna as to who was His choicest companion. He unhesitatingly called Radha's name, at which all were surprised as they had never seen her. They begged to have a glimpse of her. She was called and when she appeared with her breathtaking beauty -

"Just as a lamp or the moon appears dim before the sun, so the wives of Sri Krishna became pale or insignificant before the indescribable brilliance of Radha, like a lotus in the night."

Radha's was not selfish love. To give up this love and part from Him was inevitably a pain and and poignant sadness but she was aware that Krishna did not belong to her alone. He belonged to the world. And when the time came for Him to leave her for Mathura she unhesitatingly withdrew herself. However Krishna saw through this sacrifice the pang of separation arising out of the deep love borne by her for Him. He reassured her -

"I am in the whole world, and the whole world is in Me.
Know then, Radha, that you will always be in Me!"

And Radha was aware of it. Radha, the expression of pure and perfect love, longed to unite her soul in mystic love with Him. Krishna never forsook her. He gave her the highest place of

श्रीकृष्ण चरणाम्भोज द्वारकां वृषभानुताम् ।
भवभेदप्रमोद् वाधां राधामाराधयाम्यहम् ॥

Radha and Krishna

respect and recognition. In all *shivalas* and many other places today she stands in all her glory beside Him, watchful of His minutest care and drinking in the sweetness of His melody.

Puja

On this day, devotees after their usual worship to all the deities in the *puja* room, pay special tribute to the unalloyed love of Radha for Krishna. Women pray that the love and care they have for their husbands keep on growing unabated, and be reciprocal. They deck the couple Radha and Krishna with flowers, garlands and other ornaments. They offer fruits and *prasad*. Prayers are sung and excerpts from scriptures are read. Devotees worship Vishnu and Lakshmi too as they consider Krishna and Radha to be their *avatars*.

Shree Krishna charanaambhoja
Dwiréphaam vrishbhaanujaam.
Bhava bheda bhrmodbaadhaam
raadhaam aaraadhyaamyaham.

Anant Chaturdashi

Anant Chaturdashi is celebrated on the *chaturdashi* (fourteenth day) of the bright fortnight (*suklapaksh*) of the month of *Bhadrapad* (August/September).The festival is held in honour of Lord Vishnu who lies on the seven headed serpent, *Shesh Naga,* in the Ocean of Milk. He is also known as the *Sheshshayana,* the one who is resting on the *Shesh Naga*. His wife Lakshmi, Goddess of Luck and Wealth, is with Him massaging His feet. Sometimes Brahma the Creator is also seen in the picture. He is seated on a full-blown lotus arising from Lord Vishnu's navel. Mostly women married or unmarried attend to this festival.

अनन्त संसार महासमुद्रे मग्नं समभ्युध्दर वासुदेव ।
अनन्तरुपे विनियोजयस्व अनन्त नमो नमस्ते ॥

Legend

A story closely related with the festival is about a king and his wife Sheela. The couple was once travelling by their chariot on a visit to a neighbouring king. On the way one of the wheels of the chariot came out of the axle. They were stranded. The king went to secure help from the neighbourhood while the queen went for a stroll near a river. The queen reached a spot where devotees were celebrating the *Anant Vrat*. She inquired about the *puja,* and was told all about it.

*Ananta sansaara mahaa samudré
Maganam samabhyuddhara vaasudeva.
Ananta roopévniyojayaswa
Anant sootraaya namo namasté.*

The queen was inspired by the celebration and started performing the rituals every year. However the king was not pleased with the celebration, and insisted that the queen should give it up. Within a very short time, the king lost his kingdom and along with it all his wealth and glory. He fell ill and was among the most miserable people. The queen then pleaded with her husband to have the *puja* started anew. Both of them called at the river and began to hold the *vrat* on the *Anant Vrat* day and perform the rituals. Luck came back to them, and by the time the fourteen *vrats* were completed the king got back his realm, and all his fortune and repute.

A variation to the above is that instead of a king and his queen, the story involves Rishi Kaundiya and his wife Sushi. The *rishi* did not trust the attributes of the festival and dissuaded his wife from performing it. As a result he lost all his possession and health, and was very miserable. Lord Krishna then appeared in his dream one night and advised him to perform the *puja.* All was restored to him.

Celebrating the festival

Devotees wake up early and have a bath. They proceed to the *puja* room and do the usual cleaning. They perform all the rituals connected with welcoming the deities, and offer, among other things, betel leaves, nuts, flowers, and sundry fruits to the deities, in particular to Lord Vishnu. After the *puja* at home

Anant Chaturdashi by the riverside

devotees call at a river, a lake or seaside, - any surrounding where water in which God Vishnu resides is the prevailing agent. Together with the same offerings as in the morning devotees take along with them a roll of thread and an earthen lamp. After a bath in the river or the sea, they meet at some place on the bank where the ceremony is performed with the assistance of a *pujari* (priest).

A fake snake with seven heads is made of cloth or branches of leaves to represent the *Shesh Naga*. Rituals are performed and all the offerings are made to the *Naga*, usually on a plate with the earthen lamp lit on it. A special offering is the *pooah* made of flour. The priest recites excerpts from the *Vishnu Purana*. The ceremony is closed at about noon by performing a *hawan* (fire sacrifice) followed by devotees making some *daan* (offerings) to the *pujari* (priest). Devotees repair to their home and break their fast.

On this day women usually wear red or yellow sarees. Once devotees start this *puja* they have to perform it uninterruptedly during fourteen years. At the rituals at the river the devotees cut a piece of thread fourteen times the length of their body from the roll. They make fourteen knots on the thread and apply a tinge of milk, *abir* and *kumkum* (coloured powder). Married women dye their thread yellow while young girls keep theirs white. They offer it to the *Shesh Naga* at the time of the *puja*. Through *mantras* divine power is imparted to it. Devotees then tie it on their arms as a mark of protection.

Pitri Paksh

The *Pitri Paksh* is observed during the whole of the dark fortnight (*krishnapaksh*) of the month of *Ashvina* (September/October). During this period rituals are held to pacify the soul and beg blessings from elders who have left this world.

Tarpan

It is believed that during the *Pitri Paksh* period the souls of the departed relatives are released from their abode in heaven to come down to earth and visit their close ones. As such these ethereal bodies have to be welcomed as honoured guests. Since the very first day oblations known as *shraddas* are offered. The initial ceremony consists of offering the *tarpan*. The eldest son of the family, or any male member of the family, after taking a bath performs the rituals. Just as for most *pujas*, he first does the *sankalp* through which he identifies himself to the ethereal body. He takes betel leaves, three blades of *kush* grass, *akshat* (rice), *chandan* paste, *til* (sesame seeds) and flowers across the palm of his hands. Accompanied by *mantras* he lays them down in front of him. He then does the *tarpan* on them. Sometimes the *tarpan* is done on a stem of *peepul* sunk upright in the ground.

The devotee fills a container with water in which he drops some *akshat*, *chandan* paste, *til* and *Gangajal*. He then holds three blades of *kush* and flowers on a betel leaf across both his palms joined together (*anjouri*) to give the *tarpan*. This is done by taking water from the container with the joined palms and pouring it on the betel leaves earlier laid on the ground. The first *tarpan* is given to the Gods - Brambha, Vishnu, Rudra, Prajapate and others by facing east. The next *tarpan* is given to the sons of Brambha - Sanaka, Sanandana, Sanatana and Sanatkumara by facing north. The devotee once again turns to the east to offer *tarpan* to the *rishis* - Vasistha, Narada, Marich and others. The fourteen *yams* are next given the *tarpan* in the south. The *yams* are Yamaye, Dharmarajaye, Mrithuyuvaye, Antakaye, Vaivaswataye, Kalaye, Bhoutakshaye, Audoumaraye, Dadhnaye, Paarmashtine, Vrikodharaye, Chitraye, Chitraguptaye. The last *tarpan* is destined to the deceased parents - father considered as Vasu, grandfather as Rudra, great grand father as Aditya, mother as Gayatri, grandmother as Savitri and the great grand mother as Saraswati. Other members of the family who have passed away are also given the *tarpan*. This is done facing the south. The *tarpan* can also be done on any *amasya* day which is the darkest night of a month.

The devotee begs from Yama that the departed soul be kept in peace and in harmony with the surroundings. This ritual is performed every morning and afternoon before dusk, and other members of the family join in. When there is no male member in the family, the eldest married female member, nearest kin to the departed soul can perform the ceremony. In very orthodox families the one performing the ritual is not allowed to shave or have his hair cut or nails trimmed.

Pindam

Some time during this period a main *puja* is held with the participation of a *pujari* (priest). On this day ground rice is cooked in milk together with some *til* (sesame seeds), basil leaf, and honey. It is called *pindam* and is cooked in an earthen container on a fire mostly outside in the yard. The cooked rice is made into a number of rice balls usually seven. The first ball is for the *agni daddha*, that is, for any unknown departed soul. Out of the remaining six balls, three are meant for the male - father, grandfather and great grandfather. The remaining three are for the mother, grandmother and great grandmother. The *tarpan* is also done on that day. To close the *puja* a *hawan* (sacrificial fire) is done just as for any other *puja*. Vegetables are cooked and offered to the departed souls as *ansh*. It is believed that once the *puja* is completed and the *daan* made to the priest the departed souls would be in peace and plenty for the whole year in their blissful abode, the *pitri-loka*. However the need of this main *puja* does not arise during the course of the year if a blood member of the family has died and rituals have been performed. The *puja* is also not performed again, if during the year there has been a wedding in the family.

Jivit Putrika Vrat

The *Jivit Putika Vrat* is held on the *asthami* (eighth day) during the *Pitri Paksh* period which is the dark fortnight (*krishnapaksh*) of the month of *Ashvina* (September/October). On this day mothers keep fast and worship Lord Vishnu for the long life and welfare of their sons.

The word *putra* stands for *pu* (*narak*, hell) and *tra* (remover), that is one who removes somebody from hell or saves him from going there. Hence when somebody dies the son is called upon to perform all the rituals which are commonly known as the *karma kirya*. The rituals are done at the time of the cremation and particularly during the days that follow. When all the rituals have been ceremoniously and perfectly done, it is believed that the departing soul rests in peace far from hell. Hindus attach much importance to the birth of a son as they believe that the son keeps the family tree growing, keeps the *bansh* going. He is going to stay with the family and the family name will be kept running throughout the centuries, unlike the daughter who goes away to some other family, and adopts the name and *kool* (family) of her husband.

Legend

Once there were two sisters, Tilo and Shiyarin. They were both childless. They decided to keep fast and worship the Lord on the *Jivit Putrika Vrat* day. While Shiyarin kept her fast, Tilo was tempted by some bones and made a meal out of them secretly. After some time each gave birth to a son. Shiyarin's son was hale and hearty, intelligent and virtuous. Tilo's son was dull, weak and always ill. After some time Tilo's son died. Tilo lamented to her sister and confessed about the sin she had committed on the fasting day. Shiyarin advised her to keep the fast anew and in all its rigidity. Soon Tilo was endowed with a son as intelligent and as strong as her sister's.

In remembrance of the above sisters, devotees keeping fast for the *Jivit Putrika Vrat* prepare two *litis* (a sort of unleavened bread made with flour) on the eve. They offer the two *litis*, sugar and water to them at some clean place, usually on a lower roof of the house so that they are not eaten by animals, like stray dogs. They then go on a rigorous fast on the next day, without even taking water. They perform all the rituals connected with the fast. The next day they break the fast, after offering some *daan* to *brahmins*.

Draupadi

Lord Krishna Himself recommended Draupadi that mothers should keep this *vrat* for the welfare of their sons. The story originates from the great epic, *Mahabharata*.

The fight between the Pandavas and the Kauravas was going on. Drona who was the *guru* (teacher) of both the Pandavas and the Kauravas was fighting on the Kauravas' side. As the Pandavas could not defeat him, they resorted to a strategem. They killed the elephant Aswathama and started shouting and jubilating - "Aswathama has been killed! Aswathama is dead!" On hearing the news, Drona got upset mistaking the elephant's death to be the death of his son who bore the same name. To be confirmed of the veracity of the statement, Drona inquired from Yudhistira, eldest brother of the Pandavas and the great Upholder of Truth. The latter replied - "Yes, Aswathama the elephant is dead," but lowering his voice at the word 'elephant', thus rendering it inaudible in the uproar. Drona gave up the fight and Arjuna killed him unarmed.

In revenge Aswathama threatened to kill all the male members of the Pandava's family. He strung his bow and beheaded the five sons of Draupadi with a single arrow. Abhimanyu, the son of Arjuna and Subhadra was already killed in the battle leaving his pregnant wife Uttra in the care of Draupadi. Aswathama now even tried to kill the baby in her womb. Draupadi immediately called on Krishna who advised both Uttra and Draupadi to keep the *Jivit Putrika Vrat*. When Uttra's son was born, he was lifeless. Krishna instilled life in him as a blessing for the *vrat* kept by Uttra and Draupadi. The son later became King Parajeet.

Another legend connected with the festival is about a *brahmin* whose all children died in infancy. He felt so miserable that one day he called on Lord Krishna, who apprised him that once more his next child would die at the age of three. The *brahmin* pleaded with the Lord for some means to save his child. He was advised to perform rituals and offer prayers to the Sun-God. Once while he was in deep meditation, and performing the rituals the Sun-God was so pleased that he dropped a necklace to him. The *brahmin* was happy to have received an armour of protection.

When the child grew three years old, Yama came to take his life. The necklace responded, and Lord Krishna intervened with his *sudarshan chakra* (discus). Yama fled away leaving a shadow. The shadow was no other than the ominous Sani. The latter tried to steal the necklace and take away the protective power. Immediately the Lord appeared and threatened to destroy him. He pleaded for mercy, and spontaneously promised to help the *brahmin.* Lord Vishnu was pleased with him and gave him abode in a *peepul* (Indian holy fig) tree. Hence the belief that Sani resides in the *peepul* tree, and mothers pray to him on Saturdays when they want to seek blessings from him for their sons.

The peepul tree

Durga Navmi

The *Durga Navmi* is celebrated in honour of Mother Durga who is the consort of Shiva. The festival starts on the new moon day in the bright fortnight (*suklapaksh*) of the month of *Ashvina* (September/October) and lasts for nine days. A *Durga Navmi* is also held in the month of *Chaitra* (March/April) and is commonly known as the *Ram Navmi*. Durga is considered as the most powerful of all female deities and has 1008 names or epithets.

Mother Durga

The basic aim of the celebration is to propitiate Mother Durga as the embodiment of *shakti*, and to pray for both spiritual and material progress. She is the energy of Shiva and everything emanates from Her. Shiva is the silent witness, Durga is the wielder of power. She is usually worshipped under Her nine different names during the nine day period. They are Shailaputri, Brahmacharini, Chandraghanta, Kushmanda, Skandamata, Katyayani, Kalaratri, Mahagauri and Siddhidartri.

जयंती मंगला काली भद्रकाली कपालिनी ।
दुर्गा क्षमा शिवा धात्रि स्वाहा स्वधा नमस्तुते ॥

God is adored as the Mother for this festival, thus making it easier for the spiritual aspirant to come closer to Him through Her, the Mother. A child has more intimacy with his mother because of her kindness, loving nature, tender and affectionate looks, and he is aware that she attends to all his needs. He trusts her and obeys her, and as the days go by his trust and affection gets deeper, until finally he surrenders completely to her. Thus by praying Mother Durga the devotee reaches the Supreme Being.

The meanings and attributes of Durga are many and the devotee can worship Her in any of the manifestations that appeals most to him. She can be -

Durga	Goddess beyond Reach
Bhadrakali	The Auspicious Power of Time
Amba or Jagadamba	Mother of the World
Annapurna	Giver of Food and Plenty
Sarvamangala	Auspicious Goddess
Bhairavi	Terrible, Fearful, Power of Death
Chandika or Chandi	Violence, Wrath, Fury
Lalita	Playfulness Personified
Bhavani	Giver of Existence

Durga has two distinct personalities as one can see from the above. She is Uma the Light; Gauri, the Yellow-pigmented Beauty; Bhavani, the Giver of Existence; Jagatmata, Mother of the Universe. She is compassionate and loving to those who are righteous and divine. She is pleasant, attractive and full of care. Her maternal feelings of love and protection for the devotees go beyond bound. But to the unrighteous and the wicked She is fierce and terrible. She is Bhairavi, the Power of Death; Chandika the Violent, the Furious.

Mother Durga is also worshipped as the *Maha Maya,* which according to the gunas of nature, *Tamasic, Rajasic* and and*Satvic* take the forms of MahaKali, Maha Lakshmi and Maha Saraswati. The devotee worships Mother Kali for the first three days, Mother Lakshmi for the next three days and Mother Saraswati for the last three days. In the initial three days of the worship of Mother Kali, the lower instincts of man are burnt out He is purged out of all evils and impurities. He now acquires a spiritual personality and worships Mother Lakshmi, symbol of purity to achieve divine grace and experience bliss. The next step is to acquire knowledge, to get supreme wisdom for God realisation. He finally prays Mother Saraswati who is knowledge absolute. After these nine days of worship the devotee is set on

*Jayantee mangalaa kalee
bhadra kaalee kapaalinee.
Durgaa kshamaa shivaa dhaatree
Swaahaa swadhaa namostu té.*

the path to success on both material and spiritual planes.

Celebrating the puja

As for every major festival devotees have to keep themselves disciplined in celibacy, food and drinks. No alcoholic drink is allowed, and as regards food many go on a diet of sweet meal. Those who cannot fast, take only one meal with salt daily and everybody has to be vegetarian. After taking a bath and cleaning the house on the first day they make all the preparations.

Initially a *bedi* (altar) is made in a room where the *puja* is to be held. It should be in such a position that when the devotee is in front of it he faces east. It is decorated by having a lotus flower beautifully drawn over it. A *lota* (pot) is laid on the flower. It is filled with water. Rosewater, *Gangajal*, betel leaves and nuts, *vetiver, chiendent* and some silver coins are dropped into it. At the mouth of the pot there is the *panch palao* (five kinds of leaves) which could be any five of these - mango, *neem, bar, pankar, peepul* and *gular* leaves. These leaves are arranged in a way to have them beautifully spread out. A *katori* (cup) filled with rice is laid over the leaves. A decorated coconut is placed on the rice, and it is given all facial traits and colours. This is the *kalash* and represents Mother Durga. Sometimes the coconut and the pot are so beautifully dressed with clothing and decked

Bless me, Mother!

with jewels that together they give the look of a majestic lady in a sitting posture. The images of Mother Durga, Mother Kali, Mother Lakshmi and Mother Saraswati are placed in the background.

The Mother is considered as a cherished guest. She is given a *sari*, bangles, mirror, comb, *tiklis* and *sindrawata*.(a container having vermillion). She is offered water and even a *paan ke bhira* (made of betel leaves, nuts and other ingredients). She has a handkerchief, one end of which contains some rice, *jeera, jawain*, turmeric, betel leaf, flower, nut and silver coins - a symbol of plenty and of fulfilment. This is known as the *koncha.* She wears a beautiful garland and has a lamp fuelled with ghee and cotton wick burning night and day in front of her. There is also an earthen light on each side of her.

On the first day the devotee does the *sankalp* identifying himself to the deities and taking the vow to complete the nine day *puja* in all its austerity. Everyday offerings are made to the deity. The offerings usually consist of fruits, garlands, flowers, leaves and *prasad.* Recitations are done from the *Devi Mahatmyam* in the morning and evening. It is considered very auspicious and of great benefit to meditate daily on the *mantra* of the *Devi*. The *mantra* is "*Aim rhim cling chamundaayai vichche*'" and has to repeated 108 times through a *jap mala* (rosary).

ॐ ऐं ह्रीं क्लीं चामुणडायै विच्चै

On the ninth day the devotee prepares a special offering - *puri* and *khir*. Puri is made of flour. The devotee makes the dough, gets it broken into small balls and rolled flat into round shapes. They are fried in hot ghee. *Khir* is made of rice cooked in milk, with sugar and other ingredients added. Nine betel leaves are placed in a row in front of the Mother. A pair of *puris* with *khir*, grams, *rot, prasad*, fruits and flowers on it is laid on each leaf. These nine pairs of *puris* are meant for the nine attributes of the Mother. *Tiklis, sindoor* (vermillion) usually worn by married women, are also given to the deity. And what is most important is the *chak* which is a liquid mixture of nine cardamoms and eighteen cloves ground together. When the *puris* have been laid in front of the *Devi*, nine pieces of camphor are lit in a row. The *chak* is then poured gently going round the row of *puris* from left to right. The devotee then prostrates in front of the deity and requests for Her grace. The *chak* is then applied on the head. All other members of the family pay the same reverence. This ceremony is usually carried out by a married woman. The *chak* may be offered daily, though not the *puris* and the *khir*. The *chak* is considered very sacred and is the fulfilment of the rituals. Sometimes a *hawan* (fire worship) is performed to close the *puja*.

One pair of *puris* with *khir* and other *prasad* is also offered to each of the deities Mahakali, Maha Lakshmi and Maha Saraswati. Offerings are also made to Mother Annapurna (another manifestation of Mother Durga) and to Lord Shiva. At the two ends of the door the same offerings are made in respect of *Douar Matrika* (Mother at the Entrance). When the ceremony is completed one experiences but bliss and fulfilment all round

The assistance of a priest is vital in the performance of the Durga *puja*, at least on the first and last day. On the first day the priest sanctifies the place. He initiates and instructs the worshipper as to the way the rituals should be carried out. He invokes the deity and does the *avahan* (instils life in the *kalash*). The goddess is to reside in the *kalash* during the *navmi*. She becomes a living member of the family, and spreads Her spiritual glow all around so that the *puja* is carried out in an atmosphere of discipline and piety. At the end of the *puja* on the ninth day the priest comes again to perform the *visarjan,* sending back the goddess to Her abode.

Many devotees may not be in a position to hold the *puja* for nine days. But as the *suklapaksh* (bright fortnight) period is conducive to worship, they try to hold at least a one day *Durga Path puja*. Indeed this has become a widespread practice for the last few years in Mauritius.

The *shivalas* and marquees, put up specially in some places for the occasion, are beautifully decorated for this nine day festival. Recitations of verses from the *Devi Mahatmyam*, discourses on religious themes, devotional music and songs and reading from the Scriptures are a common feature during this period.

Devi Mahatmyam

During the nine days of the festival devotees read the *Devi Mahatmyam* which contains all the essence of the *Devi*

Bhagavatam, an entire *Purana* dedicated to Mother Durga. It is also known as the *Durgasaptasati* or *Candi* which forms part of another well-known *Purana*, the *Markandeya Purana*. The *Devi Mahatmyam* has thirteen chapters and seven hundred verses. It is an expression of deep devotional fervour, and of poetic excellence. As the story unfolds itself one gets convinced of the Mother's living presence, of Her limitless love and care to the cause of the good and the divine. Her triumph in the battle against the demoniac forces, the poetical hymns chanted by the gods and, above all, the firm assurance and blessings given by Her to the devotees inspire them with hope.

A legend which is very familiar from the *Mahatmyam* is connected with the Devi's fight against the monster Mahishasura. The demon had once defeated all the gods including Indra, Surya, Agni, Vayu, Chandra, Varuna and had taken possession of their kingdoms. He had become a terrible threat to them. All the gods then assembled and called on Brahma. The latter heading the assembled gods went to Vishnu and Shiva. They complained of the sufferings caused by Mahishasura and begged for the destruction of the demon.

Vishnu and Shiva got very angry as were Brahma and all the minor gods. From the pooling together of the powers of all the gods a very strong light sprung out, and assumed a female body. Her beauty as well as Her valour were incomparable. All the deities then provided their weapons to the form which came to be known as Durga. Shiva gave Her His trident, Vishnu His disc, Agni His spear, and all other gods many other weapons.

To beautify the goddess ornaments and jewels were provided. The milk ocean gave Her a necklace, earrings, bracelets, a brilliant halfmoon, armlets, anklets, rings, and a garland of unfading lotuses for Her head and breasts. With a defying laugh She gave a loud roar which frightened the wicked Mahishasura and his army. The generals accompanied by all the soldiers of Mahisasura's army advanced to fight Mother Durga, who putting up a strong fight destroyed them all. Then Mahishasura himself came forward in his buffalo form. The Goddess mounted Her lion and bounced on him. The demon assumed several bodies trying to confuse the Devi. At last after taking a cup of honeyed wine She summoned up all Her might. She pinned him down with Her foot on his neck and pierced him to death. She is since then also known as Mahishasuramardini.

Another instance portraying her prowess is Her fight against the two demon brothers, Sumbha and Nishumbha and their armies. These demons had taken over all the kingdoms of the gods who fled to the Himalayas. There, through the chanting of the hymn, *Aparajit-stotra* (The Unconquered) supplicated the Mother for help. The Mother manifested Herself as Kaushika emanating from the body of Parvati, who after the manifestation became Kali. In the fight that followed between the demons' armies and Mother Kaushika, a very fierce demon Raktabeeja, put up a tough resistance to Her. Wherever drops of blood fell on the ground from his body, numberless demons of his size and strength came to life. They fought against the Devi. Mother Kaushika then invoked Kali from Her forehead and requested Her to drink the drops of blood coming from Raktabeeja's body. When he was emptied of all his blood She struck him to death. Sumbha and Nishumba gave way to unbounded wrath when Raktabeeja was killed. They faced the Devi in a number of ways and with limitless weapons. But the Devi as usual proved too strong, and destroyed both of them, thus restoring peace and freedom to the gods and to the world.

Once two demons Madhu and Kaitaba sprang out from the dirt of Vishnu's ears while He was asleep and threatened to kill Brahma. The latter invoked Her as the *Maha Maya* who came out from Vishnu's eyes, mouth, nostril, arms, heart and breast. She responded by awakening Vishnu. The latter put up a fight and killed the demons whom She betwitched through Her *maya*.(illusive power). Mother Durga is also known as Chamunda for having killed the demons Chanda and Munda, as Nanda for having predicted the death of the demon king Kansa by Krishna, as Sakhambari Mata for protecting the world from a famine, and as Kumari the Eternal Virgin.

Once the deity had to fight for nine days and nine nights to defeat Bhandasura and his forces. Lord Shiva had burnt Kamdeva with the fire of His third eye. Ganesha, playfully moulded a figure out of the ashes, and His father Lord Shiva instilled life into it. The figure became the terrible demon Bhandasura after acquiring a boon from Lord Shiva for severe penances performed. He and his forces began oppressing all people and soon became a threat to the world. The Divine

Mother then had to fight against him for nine days. She was victorious on the tenth day which is known as the *Vijaya Dasami*. To celebrate the *Vijaya Dasami* a *Kanya puja* is performed. It involves having nine litle girls worshipped as the embodiment of the Divine Mother. They are donned with new clothes, ornaments and gifts, and are fed sumptuously.

Bidaye

An inspiring legend is connected with Mother Durga. The Mother of Durga, Mena, longed to see her daughter. Lord Shiva granted Her leave to spend some days with Her parents. During Her stay Mena and her husband Himavat spoilt Her with utmost care, love and affection as befitted the occasion when a married daughter visited her parents. They often locked Her in embrace recalling the days of her childhood. After spending nine days in the warm and loving company of Her parents Durga had to return home. The parting was very painful and Durga broke into spasms of weeping. Her parents became helpless and with tears trickling into the creases of their cheeks had to do the *bidaye* (send off) in spite of themselves. The send off was done in great pain but with much affection and ceremony. The celebration of the *Navratri* reflects the affectionate and ceremonious moods of the Mother's visit to the devotee's house with the *bidaye* on the ninth day.

Indeed, in some cities in India, it has become a tradition for married daughters to call on their parents during these nine days. The whole family performs the *Durga Puja* together. And all the members consider Mother Durga as a daughter visiting them. The family performs the *puja* for nine days giving the Mother a warm welcome and high regard consistent with the visit of a cherished guest. On the last day they take the image to the river with all ceremony associated with a daughter's departure for her husband's house. The same love and reverence are then paid to their daughters when they leave their parents for their in-laws at the end of the nine day *puja*.

Vijay Dashmi

Vijay Dashmi is celebrated on *dashmi* (tenth day), that is, the day following the *Durga Navmi* which is held in the bright fortnight (*suklapaksh*) of the month of *Ashvina* (September/October). It is considered as the day of victory. Mother Durga had to fight during nine days to be able to vanquish the demons Mahishshura, Dhumrochana, Canda, Munda, Raktabeeja, Sumbha, and Nisumbha. The devoties were relieved after the defeat of the demons, and offered prayers on the *dashmi*, the day of victory. The *Vijay Dashmi* is also held in honour of Lord Rama. During the fight against Ravana He worshipped Mother Durga for nine days of the *Navratri*. He faced Ravana on the tenth day (*dashmi*), and was able to defeat him. The *Vijay Dashmi* is very auspicious and is considered to be the best day to embark on any project.

In India sometimes during the *Navratri puja* a pitcher full of incense and scented water is placed in front of a *Brahma* image made of one hundred *dharba* grass. On the tenth day, the *Vijay Dashmi*, the pot is removed. The priests or *brahmins*, go from house to house and bless the residents by sprinkling the holy water. The residents receive them with fruits, flowers and *daan*.

A ritual connected with the *Vijay Dashami* is the *Sabaratsava*.. The *Puranas* mention that after worshipping Mother Durga during the nine days with various offerings, the devotee should then immerse Her image in the river on the *dashmi*. The auspicious time is when the moon is in conjunction with the *Sravana* constellation.

Karak Chaturthi Vrat

The *Karak Chaturthi Vrat* festival, commonly known as *Karwa Chaut*, is held on the *chaturthi* (fourth day) of the dark fortnight *(krishnapaksh)* of the month of *Kartika* (October/November). It is observed by married women whose husbands are still alive. Widows and unmarried girls are not allowed to celebrate it.

Celebrating the festival

On this day women wake up early and take a bath in the very early hours of the day. They wear new clothes, jewelry and adorn themselves by applying *sindoor* (vermillion) as commendable to all married women. They collect various articles for performing the rituals, in particular ten *karwas* (earthen pots with sprouts) and ten lamps. The *karwas* are decorated with a paste of coloured rice. Sketches of *karwas,* sun and moon are beautifully drawn on the floor. The devotees then worship Mother Parvati, Her consort Shiva and their two sons Kartikaya and Ganesha. The *puja* can be performed either alone or in groups, at home or in the *mandir*, or at such places as on the river bank. They pray for their husbands' long life, welfare and prosperity, and wish that they be a united and happy family as Mother Parvati's. At night when the moon appears they give the *arag* with water, flowers and other articles and see their husbands' face. They revere their husbands. They spoil them by garlanding them, washing their feet, waving light in front of the face to protect them from *nazar* (evil eye), and feeding them with sweets. They seek the blessings of the elderly. Parents and all elderly members of the family bless their married children and present them with gifts as new clothes, jewelry and sweetmeals together with the blessed *karwas* and *deepaks* (lamps).

Legend

Once a married princess was spending some days at her parents' residence. It was the *Karwa Chaut*, and after observing the rituals she broke the fast. Just then she received news of her husband's death. Wailing she repaired to her husband's house. On her way she met Mother Parvati. The princess could not help from acquainting the goddess of her husband's demise. Mother Parvati, of overwhelming sensibility and sympathy, and being aware that she had kept the fast responded by cutting Her finger and giving her a few drops of Her blood. She recommended her to anoint the body of her husband with it. She did accordingly. The prince immediately came back to life.

A slight variation to the legend is that while keeping the fast on this day, the princess got exhausted due to the austerity of the rituals. She fainted. Her parents and relatives produced a fake moon by lighting a fire on a hill top. The princess, at the appearance of the fake moon, broke her fast. As soon as she took the first morsel, news came of her husband's death. She immediately left for the king's palace when on the way she met Mother Parvati and Lord Shiva. She apprised them of her unfortunate plight. Mother Parvati came to know that she had broken the fast through no fault of hers. She gave her some drops of blood from Her finger. The princess rubbed the blood on her husband's body, and the latter was brought back to life.

The story is also connected with another woman called Virawatee. She kept fast on the *Karwa Chaut,* but could not stand the austerity of the fast. Her brother produced a fake moon and had her break the fast earlier. Almost immediately news came of her husband's death. She started crying when Lord Indra's wife, Sachi called on her. Sachi who knew all about what had happened recommended her to hold the *puja* anew. And when Virawatee gave the *arag* in the evening at the appearance of the moon, her husband came back to life.

The festival also originates from another legend. Sage Bhrigu used to worship Lord Shiva and was so fanatical in his devotion that he refused to honour Parvati on the same level. Parvati merged Herself into the body of Shiva, who thus became *Ardhanavisvara* (half-man, half-woman). Even then he refused, and bored through the centre by becoming a *bringa* (bee) to complete his circumambulation. Parvati kept the *Dedara Vrat* in protest. Shiva agreed to have Parvati's right established. He got Bhrigu to realise his mistake.

It is believed that the festival gathered momentum in the times of uninterrupted warfare in some parts of India. There were heavy losses of life. As a result women celebrated it widely and prayed for the victory and safe return of their husbands.

Hoi

A festival somewhat similar is the *Hoi* celebrated on the *asthami* (eighth day) of the dark fortnight (*krishnapaksh*) of *Kartika* (October/November), that is, four days after the *Karwa Chaut*. While for the *Karwa Chaut* women fast for the sake of their husbands, here they fast for the welfare and fulfilment of their children, in particular for their sons. It is considered a very auspicious day for married women to pray for a son if they do not have one.

Dhana Teras

The *Dhana Teras* is observed two days before the *Divali* festival which is held on the *amavasya* (darkest night) of the dark fortnight of the month *Kartika* (October/November). The festival is held in honour of the physician of the gods, Dhanwantari, and the God of Wealth, Kuber. A fast is kept until the evening. The festival is celebrated with a view to acquiring health and wealth which are the basic needs of man. Many also offer prayers to the God of Death, Yama, on this day.

Performing the puja

After a bath the devotee performs some rituals in his *puja ghar* or in a clean corner of his house. A *thali* (metal plate) is filled with coloured (pink) rice. Four flowers are laid at the four corners, to represent the cardinal points. A *lota* (pot) decorated with *abir*, *kumkum*, *sindoor* (coloured powder), is filled with water, and a bunch of mango leaves is placed at the mouth with the leaves beautifully spread out. Flowers, *akshat* (rice) and some coins are dropped in the *lota* as a sign of auspiciousness. A *katori* (cup) filled with rice is laid over the mouth of the pot. On the *katori* an earthen lamp fuelled with ghee is lit. The lamp has to be kept burning for three days till *Divali* night. The light from this lamp is used to light the *Divali* lamps. Prayers in honour of the gods, main among whom Kubera, are sung As from this day utensils, clothes, and everything needed in connection with the celebration of *Divali* is purchased. Some use the light of this lamp to make *kaajal* which is applied to the eyes to beautify them and to protect the eyesight.

Dhanwantari is believed to have compiled the *Ayur Veda*, the Scripture which deals with medicine. He is the one who brought the container of *amrit* from the ocean while it was being churned (*sagarmantham*) by the *devtas* and *asuras* together, and his coming out of the sea has earned him the epithet of *Sudha Pani* (Clean Water). He is said to have been born as the King of Kasi and brought medical science to the earth. His seat is in front of

धनाध्यक्षाय देवाय नरायवो वेशिने ।
नमस्ते राजराजाय कुवेराय महात्मने ॥

Kubera, God of Wealth

Lord Vishnu's insignia, and is very handsome. He could have been a deity of the Vedic era as the *Vedas* do mention of a Dhanvantari, a god associated with herbs and medicines.

A particular event is that the housewives light a lamp, made of flour and using four wicks, at the main gate of the yard. The fast is broken in the evening.

Legend

Once Yama was holding a meeting with his *dutas* (messengers) in his dominion to listen to their grievances. Though they were more or less happy with their assignment and complied with their responsibilities, yet they said they found it very hard to cope with, in particular when they had to take the life of very young people. To support their grievances they related to him the death of a young prince.

Once a king called Hans set out on a game of hunting in a far away forest. In the hot pursuit of a very attractive deer he soon lost his way. At the end of what seemed to be an endless search to find the way back he landed in the territory of King Sashak. The latter befriended him and invited him to spend some days at his place. Meanwhile the wife of King Sashak gave birth to a

*Dhanaadhyakshaaya devaaya
nara yaanopaveshiné
Namasté raajaraajaaya kuberaaya
mahaatmané.*

very lovely son. As was the practice an astrologer was consulted for the performance of ceremonies connected with the birth. The astrologer, while reading from his *panchang* informed them that the prince would die four days after the wedding. Consequently King Hans advised his friend to have the prince taken to a lonely residence in a remote place on the bank of the river Yamuna. As a result the prince would only be surrounded by his guards, and visits from foreigners in particular of women, would be most unlikely.

The baby soon grew up into a very handsome man. One day King Hans's daughter during his visit to King Sashak went out to visit the countryside with her friends. In their quest for adventure they went far far away when they reached the prince's residence. She met the prince. It was love at first sight. To avoid any possible opposition from their parents, they got married secretly. On the fourth day after their wedding, the *dutas* came down to take the prince's life. Seeing the innocent lovely couple in their prime of youth, and the love that each had for the other, the *dutas* were sorrow-stricken. They felt disappointed of the nature of their duties.

While relating the above the *dutas* broke into tears. Yama then decreed the rule that all people who would celebrate the *Dhana Teras* with all due ceremony would be spared of an untimely death. The *dutas* were all too happy of the announcement.

Narak Chaturdashi Yam

The *Narak Chaturdashi Yam* festival is celebrated on the eve of the Divali day, which is in the month of *Kartika* (October/November). It is held to propitiate the blessings of Yama, the God of Death so that the departed souls rest in peace. A fast is kept on this day. Being *chaturdashi* of the dark fortnight (*krishnapaksh*), it may also be the *Shivaratri* day and therefore another reason to keep fast. Devotees take a bath with oil and a special grass known as the *chirchiriya* grass in bhojpuri.

Puja

A suitable spot is identified in the southern corner of the yard. The place is cleaned and coated with a paste of cowdung. *Betel* leaves are spread in a row and fourteen lamps are laid on the leaves. They are lit. It is believed that only darkness prevails in Hell, and and that the burning lamps on earth will spread light there. On receiving the light the departed souls feel happy and relieved. In response they shower blessings on those who perform the ceremony. It is also believed that this light will enlighten the path of the devotee who is performing the ritual if ever he happens to be there after his death.

The Guardian of Hell is worshipped with white flowers. Sometimes an additional lamp with four wicks is also lit for the departed elders who are there. The prayer is to request peace and light for the residents from the fourteen *yams* (guardians) of the place. And when any *puja* or *hawan* is performed in this connection the guardians are propitiated and given *tarpan* as follows - (i) Om Yamaye Namah (ii) Om Dharmarajaye Namah (iii) Om Mrithuve Namah (iv) Om Antakaye Namah (v) Om Vevasthaye Namah (vi) Om Kalaye Namah (vii) Om Sarva Bhoutakshaye Namah (viii) Om Audoumbaraye Namah (ix) Om Dadhnaye Namah (x) Om Nilaye Namah (xi) Om Paarmashtine Namah (xii) Om Vikrodharaye Namah (xiii) Om Chitraye Namah (xiv) Om Chitraguptaye namah.

The *mantra* in connection with this ritual is -

*" Om asi yamo ashya didya arvan nasi trito guyhena vratena,
yasi somena samaya viprikta ahuste trinhini divi bandhanani."*

Legend

Once there lived a very *daani* (merciful and virtuous) king called Rantidev. At the time of death, he was surprised to see Yama, God of Death coming to take him to hell. When he inquired for the reason, he was told that he once committed a sin by forgetting to receive a *brahmin* with all due honour and respect. He pleaded with Yama to extend his life on earth by one year.

The king taking his wife and only son made for the forest. On the way they met some *rishis* to whom they related their misfortune. The *rishis* advised them to perform austerities in honour of Lord Vishnu. Wasting themselves both in body and mind, and staying without food they underwent severe penances for forty-nine days. On the fiftieth day the king went to the already harvested fields to collect some grains. He could hardly get enough to prepare a meagre meal.

When the meal was ready, they made three shares out of it. Just as they were about to take their food, a hungry *brahmin* came and begged for food. The king immediately gave him his share. As soon as they started anew for their meal, a starving hunter and his dog called for rescue. The king handed over the queen's share to them. And finally when the son started his meal a collapsing woodcutter presented himself and asked for some food to save himself. He partook the son's share. Though deprived of their meal yet the three souls were happy of still being able to stick to their virtue as *daani.* Just then appeared a triad of gods who revealed themselves as Brahma, Vishnu and Mahesh. They informed the king that they themselves came to him disguised as the *brahmin*, hunter and woodcutter to put to test his faith and virtues. They were highly pleased with his devotion. They conferred on the king and his family long life, material and spiritual grace, and paved the way to *Vaikunth* on their death.

Choti Deepawali

The *Narak Chaturdashi Yam* is also known as the *Choti Deepawali*. A lamp with four wicks is first lit. Then sixteen other lamps are lit in honour of the sixteen *kalas* (powers) of Lord Krishna. Some recommend the lighting of twenty one earthen lamps. The lamps are then moved to all the rooms in the house. Lord Ganesha, Mother Lakshmi, Mother Saraswati and other gods are also worshipped with various offerings.

Divali

Divali, the festival of lights, is held on the *amasvasya* day (the darkest night) in the dark fortnight (*krishnapaksh*) of the month of *Kartika* (October/November). Divali originates from the Sanskrit word *deepawalee* which means a row of light. As such it is a festival where light predominates. - light which brings in its trail knowledge, wisdom, luck and success. Every house is lit - big or small, rich or poor, new or old. An infectious mood of joy, mirth and merriment prevails. It is the festival dedicated to the Goddess of Wealth, Mahalakshmi, who is believed to come down to earth. She roams about in every house to bestow her light, liveliness and fortune. This day, according to the *Vikram Samvatsar*, marks the beginning of the new Indian calendar. The Vikram era starts as from the reign of King Vikramaditya. It is a day when the business community starts with new account books. On this day many people pray the tools they use to earn their living.

Preparing for the festival

The festival is preceded by days of thorough cleaning. People start cleaning the house, the compound, and indeed everything

Cleaning to welcome Mother Lakshmi

they possess. The utensils are given a thorough wash, the furniture is made glossy. New clothes are made. Every nook and corner is made neat and spotlesssly clean. It is believed that if a house is left dirty and dark, it will instead be visited by Goddess Lakshmi's sister, Jyeshtha Devi and would spell misery, ruin and misfortune. Hence the painstaking cleaning to invite and receive Goddess Lakshmi only. Cleaning does not confine itself to the body only but to the inner spirit as well so that all gloom and ignorance are dispelled.

Ingredients are purchased for the making of a variety of cakes. Sweet cakes are mostly prepared ranging from the simple *ladoo*

Cooking prasad and cakes

to the painstaking *mewa samosa* through the *barfi.* Some cakes are kept to be offered to the deities. The remaining cakes are shared with relatives, neighbours and visitors. Some people call at the *ashrams*, hospitals, and charitable institutions to make donations and to share with the inmates the warmth and the light of the festival. Earthen lamps and candle sticks are purchased. To protect the light of the earthen lamps and candle sticks from being blown out by the gusts of wind, structures with bamboo stems and coloured paper are made in various designs and placed in the compound. The yards are also decorated affectionately with coloured powder (*rangoli*). Many people have their houses adorned with electric lights. Of late it has become a practice for the Municipalities of the whole island to have the public places, main streets and buildings lit in excellent settings. Special activities are organised. The big commercial firms add to the glamour of the *fete* by displaying impressive colourful boards with "*Divali Abhinandan.* Happy Divali !" In fact the festival assumes the level of national celebration. Some Catholic churches celebrate a mass on this occasion. When all is tuned, and the twilight creeps in one has the feeling of landing in the realm of *Mille et Une Nuits*.

Origin of the Festival

The festival is linked with Lord Rama, Lord Krishna, Indra, Swami Dayanand, Lord Mahavira and others. The most popular is the legend connected with Lord Rama's return from Lanka after defeating the demon king Ravana. The forces of evil had been conquered, and people were relieved of all miseries. They felt happy, and their joy and success were expressed in spreading light all around.

Another legend is linked with the killing of the demon Naraksura, the demon-king of Pragjotishpura in Assam by Satyabhama, one of Lord Krishna's consorts. Naraka, as the name implies was as terrible as hell. His tyranny knew no bounds. He had abducted thousands of women. Satyabhama came to their rescue, killed Naraka and set the country at peace. To commemorate the event people light lamps and express their feelings of joy and happiness. Many believe Krishna Himself killed the demon.

Still another legend, and this one is connected with Goddess Lakshmi whom Bali took as a prisoner. Bali was the grandson of Prahlada and had become King of the *asuras* by vanquishing all the gods. He had spread his dominion over the three worlds. Indra accompanied by all other gods appealed to Vishnu for the destruction of Bali. The Lord responded to their prayers by taking *avatar* as a *Vamana* (dwarf) in the house of the brahmin, Kashyap. One day Bali was holding a sacrifice to which Vishnu was invited. Bali was a great *daani* (donor) and would never refuse any request, particularly on the day he was holding the sacrifice. Vishnu seized the opportunity to request Bali to grant him enough space for three strides. Bali, taking it to be a joke, agreed spontaneously to the demand. Vishnu took two strides and covered the three spheres - land, sky and the ocean. Finding no room for the third stride, Bali offered Him his head. The Lord stepped over it, and he was driven to Patala - the nether region. It was the only kingdom which was henceforth left for him. Thus the Lord saved the gods, and rescued Lakshmi. The gods feeling relieved and happy celebrated the event by having light spread everywhere.

The festival

Just before dusk all devotees make for the *puja* room The images are profusely decorated with leaves and flowers, and garlanded. In keeping with the *sohraso pachar pujanam,* devotees welcome and make offerings as *prasad*, flowers and fruits to the deities in particular to Maha Lakshmi. A new lamp is lit in the *puja* room, the old one is removed. Prayers in honour of Maha Lakshmi are chanted, and excerpts from the *Devi Mahatmyam* are read. Maha Kali, Maha Saraswati and Lord Ganesha are also ceremoniously worshipped. All the earthen lamps are lit if possible in the *puja* room. Each room is supplied with at least one light to welcome Maha Lakshmi. The other earthen lamps and candles are laid on the window sills, verandahs and other corners so as to make the house bright and beautiful.

The lights soon invade the compound. Young and old, men and children all get busy lighting the lamps, and having them beautifully laid out. The decorative electric lights set up for the occasion are switched on. The blend of the rustic softness of the earthen light and the effervescence of the electric bulbs, uncommonly impressive in their unity and life, bristles all things animate and inanimate with joy and emotion. Soul-stirring *divali* songs fill the air. Devotees call on one another with assorted cakes. Children set upon lighting the the fire-works (crackers, sticks, rockets and squibs) which give an spectacular effect and add to the glamour of the celebration. The streets are thronged with people. Cars with their curio passengers make their way to the various towns and main villages to bathe in the joy and wonders of the *fete*.

Govardhan Puja

The *Govardhan* festival is celebrated on the *pratibada* (first day) of the bright fortnight (*suklapaksh*) of the month of *Kartika* (October/November), the day after *Divali*. It is held in honour of Krishna who lifted the mountain Govardhan found near Brindaban. He maintained it on his little finger for seven days to shelter the inhabitants against the flood caused by Indra, God of Heaven and Rain. This event earned Krishna the epithet of *Govardhandhari*. This festival is mostly celebrated in India.

On this day devotees keep fast and worship Krishna. They spend a night of vigil chanting praises and prayers, and offer fifty-six varieties of food to Krishna. After the *puja* the food is distributed among the devotees as *prasad*.

Origin

Indra was considered as the deity of Vraj. All the inhabitants led by Nanda paid reverence to him as he had apprised them that he was instrumental for all the benefits they were enjoying. Once, on hearing about it, Krishna dissuaded them from worshipping Indra in favour of the mountain Govardhan. He stressed that it was Govardhan who was providing shelter and food to people and animals alike. And when the worship was started for the Govardhan mountain Krishna disguising Himself partook all the offerings. This instilled a still deeper faith in Krishna's advocacy for the worship of Govardhan. Indra got furious at this instigation and promised to avenge himself. He brought about a cloud-burst which flooded the village for several days. The inhabitants got helpless and appealed to Krishna. The latter lifted the mountain and held it up it for days over the village to protect the inhabitants against the heavy rains. Indra then realised that Krishna was no other than the Supreme Being, and prostrated before Him.

Yam Dwitiya Bhaiya Duja

The *Yam Dwitiya Bhaiya Duja* is celebrated on the *dwitrya* (second day) of the bright fortnight (*suklapaksh*) of the month of *Kartika* (October/November), on the day following the *Govardhan puja*. The festival has its origin from the deep affection that Yami had for her brother Yama.

On this day the sister prepares food for her brother, and have him take the food on the bank of the river Yamuna. She prays to Yama, God of Death, for the long life, happiness and welfare of her brother. The brother reciprocates the wishes to her and her husband, and obliges her with presents and sweets.

In some villages in India the sister applies saffron and rice grains on the forehead of the brother to wish him long life, success and happiness. Some apply a paste of vermillion instead. The sister then waves light in front of the brother to protect him from what is called *nazar* (evil eye). The brother responds with presents.

Yama and Yami

Yama and Yami were twins born to Surya, the Sun-God and his wife Samjna. Once Surya fell in love with another woman, Cchaaya, who was so close in resemblance to Samjna that it was almost impossible for anybody to distinguish between the two. Soon Samjna grew tired of her husband's unbecoming behaviour. She went away from the house leaving her shadow which in all physical likeness was Cchaaya. Surya unaware of the happening had no ground for suspicion. One day, the child Yama inadvertently stepped on his mother (Cchaaya) who was hit by his leg. She instantly pronounced a curse on the child that he would lose his leg and become lame. Surya overheard the curse and realising that a mother would never curse her child grew suspicious of the identity of the mother. He went away to bring back the real mother Samjna, and to apologise to her for his unseemly behaviour.

Meanwhile Yama and Yami left the house. Yama soon grew up and founded his kingdom, the Yamraj. Yami after a very long journey reached the Golokh. The days rolled on, when one day Yama felt a very strong desire to see his sister. He set out to look for her and after a long search met her in Golokh. Yami welcomed her brother with lots of affection and warmth. She spoilt him in a number of ways, and when the time came for parting Yama wished to confer a boon on her. The sister, in remembrance of the love that she felt for her brother, requested the boon that all sisters celebrating the festival *Yam Dwitiya Bhaiya Duja* should be ensured of their brothers' health, welfare and long life.

Yami came down to earth as the sacred river Yamuna to allow brothers and sisters to meet on its banks to celebrate the festival.

Surya Chat Vrat

The *Surya Chat Vrat* is held on the *shashti* (sixth day) in the bright fortnight (*suklapaksh*) of the month of *Kartika* (October/November). As such it is held after *Divali*, and it lasts for three days from the fifth to the seventh day of the bright fortnight.

Puja

Devotees should have taken their last meal (sweetmeal) before sunset on the *panchami*, that is, on the eve of the *vrat*. They take a bath and clean the *puja* room. They pray the Sun before sunset. Afterwards they spend some time reading from the Scriptures. On the next day, the *shashti*, the devotees wake up early, have a bath again and do their *puja*. They perform all rituals in praise of the Sun-God and give the *arag*. They keep fast and spend the day by doing *japa*, meditation, and recitations from Scriptures. On the day following the *shashti* devotees after their usual *puja* go out to seek the *darshan* (blessings) of the Sun-God. They take water, *til* (sesame seeds) and some *tulsi* (holy basil) leaves in the palm of the right hand. They recite the *mantra* - "*Om Namoh Narayana'*" for Lord Vishnu with the offerings, and sip the water with reverence. They make some *daan* to *brahmins* and break their fast. The festival is celebrated mainly by mothers for the welfare of their sons. Those who long to have a child, in particular a son, also perform this *puja*.

On this day sometimes the mother takes as many kinds of vegetables and fruits as possible and goes to the seaside or to the river before sunrise. She is accompanied by her son or any boy. The ritual consists of offering all the vegetables and fruits - a symbol of youth and health - to the Sun-God and see the face of the son immediately after the prayers. Silence and discipline being the discipline of the mind, the devotee has to keep away from the din and bustle of the daily chores during the days of fasting. She observes silence as much as possible and even has her meals (sweet) in some remote corner. This helps her to concentrate on the rituals and worship.

Legend

A story connected with the *Vrat* is that once a man, Mahipal through his pride and behaviour insulted the Sun. As a result he became blind, and felt miserable. Finally he was so depressed that he wanted to commit suicide. Sage Narada appeared. He asked Mahipal to beg for forgiveness from the Sun-God and to observe the fast. Soon his eyesight was restored and he became one of the happiest souls.

Another story concerns a barren woman who longed to have a son. She sought advice from a *rishi* who recommended her to keep the *Surya Chat Vrat*. She gave herself the promise that she would keep the *Surya Chat Vrat* throughout her life if she begot a son. The days rolled on and after some time a lovely son was born to her. She became one of the happiest mothers, and taken up with joy and glory she soon forgot all about her promise. The son grew up into a young and handsome man and got married to a very beautiful girl. The mother was still happier with the size of the family growing bigger. One day the couple was roaming in the forest when they were attacked by a dacoit. The latter killed the husband and took away the wife. On hearing of the mishappening the mother started lamenting. She immediately called on the *rishi* again to apprise him of her misfortune. The *rishi*, through his third eye came to know at once that the Sun-God Himself had come in the garb of a dacoit to take away the life of the son. The *rishi* reminded the woman of her promise to the Sun. She took up her vow again and started holding the fast. Within a few years her son and daughter-in-law came back to her.

Prabhodini Ekadashi

Ekadashi vrats (fasts), as one is aware, are observed by devotees on the *ekadashi* (eleventh day) of every fortnight in honour of Lord Vishnu. The *Prabhodini Ekadashi* is held on the *ekadashi* of the bright fortnight (*suklapaksh*) of the month of *Kartika* (October/November), and is another such *vrat* when strictly nothing is taken. It is considered as the most important and auspicious festive day in honour of Lord Vishnu, just as the *MahaShivaratri* is for Lord Shiva. This *ekadashi* is also known as the *Devothani Ekadashi*. The observances have to be very strict and austere. In addition to completely abstaining from food, devotees have to spend the whole day and night chanting, reading and meditating on Lord Vishnu. The benefits derived from the fast are great, as great as those derived by holding the *Aswamedha Yajna* (horse sacrifice).

It is believed that Lord Vishnu sleeps during the rainy season, from the month of *Asadha* (June/July) to the *ekadashi* of *Kartika* (October/November). Others say that after His tough fight against the demon Shankeshasura, the Lord got very tired and needed a long rest. And still another reason for Lord Vishnu going for a long slumber of four months is that Goddess Lakshmi was not pleased with Her Lord's response to Sage Bhrigu and left Him for some time. Lord Vishnu went on meditation during this period until His consort came back. And along with Him all the other deities too went for a long slumber. In India the deities are awakened on this day by beating a big metal plate with a sugarcane stick chanting "*Utho Devo, Jago Devo*" (Wake up and rise, Oh Gods!)

Puja

As usual after taking a bath and cleaning the *puja* room, devotees perform rituals by offering *prasad*, flowers and the first products of the harvest such as sugarcane, potatoes and fruits. Special offerings for the occasion are mango buds, *laurier* flowers, *tulsi* leaves and the *durva* grass. They recite prayers to the gods and goddesses, in particular to Lord Vishnu and Mother Lakshmi. They keep a night of vigil usually at the *shivalas* where *kirtans* and *bhajans* are chanted. The *pujari* reads from the *Mahatam Katha,* and discourses on the Lord's good deeds. The fast is broken on the next day, after taking the *panchamrita*. It is said that none should eat rice on this day as the eaten seeds turn into worms from the curse given to a demon by Brahma. This day is considered very auspicious for growing the holy basil plant of which Lord Vishnu is very fond.

Origin

Sage Bhrigu was once entrusted by the *devas* with the task of ascertaining the genial qualities of the gods who deserved the highest praise. Bhrigu first called on Brahma who was discoursing to His disciples on the *Vedas*. He was eulogising His own achievements as the originator of those learned scripts, and did not pay the respect due to him as a *brahmin*. He left, cursing Him that He would not be worthy of the highest worship. The sage next went to Lord Shiva. In spite of having waited for long, Lord Shiva still did not turn up as He was engaged in an amorous sport with Parvati. He left Shiva cursing Him that he would not be worshipped in His human form, but rather in His phallic form, the *lingam*. Finally he reached Lord Vishnu. The latter was sleeping and His consort Lakshmi was massaging His feet. Not seeing any response he kicked Him on the chest. The Lord consequently woke up and pressing the feet of the sage to His chest, asked him whether his feet were not hurt by the hardness of His body. Bhrigu was greatly impressed by Lord Vishnu's humility. He declared to the deities that Lord Vishnu deserved the highest worship.

The origin of the festival is also connected with King Rugmorgada. A young lovely woman, Mohini, tried to seduce the king and have him take his meal on this fasting day. The king aware of the fast, and to avoid being tempted, prayed fervently to Lord Vishnu. The king's prayer was answered. The Lord Himself came and whisked him off to His abode in *Vaikuntha*. Later the king came to know that Mohini was but the Lord himself who had come to test the king's faith and devotion to God. Hence those celebrating this fast with all due ceremony are released from the cycle of birth and death and attain *moksha*.

Another legend is from the *Bhagavad Purana*. One day king Ambarisha after the observances of the festival was about to break his fast when sage Durvasa called on him. The king welcomed the sage and invited him with all due respect to share the meal with him. The sage responded positively to the request. However he informed the king that he would first go for a bath to the nearby river, and requested to wait for him to take the meal. The king waited for a long time for the *rishi*, but he did not turn up. The king was getting delayed as the auspicious time *(muhurtta)* for breaking the fast was about to elapse. The king was rather confused as whether to wait for the sage or have his meal in order not to negate the effect arising from the fast. Finally he respectfully paid homage to the Lord, broke the fast by sipping some *panchamrit* (offering to God and taken by the disciples after the rituals) in the palm of his hand. The sage, through his divine eye, saw the king. On his return he cursed him and produced a demon from a hair of his to kill the king. Lord Vishnu intervened instantly. His discus beheaded the demon and pursued the sage who had to implore for pardon both from the Lord and the king.

A story connected with *ekadashis* is about the demon Muru. Once the demon was committing untold atrocities to both gods and human beings. The help of Lord Vishnu was sought. He met the demon in a very fierce fight for a very long time, but could not defeat him. He felt tired and retired. The *shakti* from Him then took over. She defeated the demon in a very short time. It is said that the *shakti* who opposed the demon was no other than His own partner, Maha Lakshmi. Lord Vishnu was much pleased with His consort. He decreed that anybody keeping fast on this *ekadashi* would reap the benefits of a *Aswamedha Yajna*.

Vaikunth Chaturdashi

The *Vaikunth Chaturdashi* fast is held on the *chaturdashi* (fourteenth day) of the bright fortnight (*suklapaksh*) of the month of *Kartika.* (October/November). While on the *Narak Chaturdashi* day devotees propitiate the blessings of Yama, Lord of Death, on the *Vaikunth Chaturdashi* day they seek the blessings of Lord Vishnu. They worship Him by lightinhg a lamp of four wicks and with offerings like flowers, fruit, *til* (sesame seeds) and *tulsi* (holy basil) leaves.

Legend

Once Sage Narada, after roving round the universe, reached Lord Vishnu's abode (*Vaikunth* - abode without thorns). He saw that only those people who were close to Him could find shelter there. The sage was surprised and pointed out to Lord Vishnu that the policy was not in keeping with His title - *Kripanidhan* (The Merciful). In response to this observation, the Lord established the rule that all those praying Him and performing rituals for His sake on the *Vaikunth Chaturdashi* day would have easy access to His abode on their death. He ordered His two gate-keepers Jay and Vijay to leave the gates of Vaikunth open to all devotees on this day.

Ganga Snan

गंगे ममाग्रतो भूञा गंगे मे देवी पृछत: ।
गंगे मे पाश्वयोर्गहि त्वयि गंगेस्तु मे स्थिति: ॥

*Gangé mamaagrato bhooyaa
Gangé mé devi prishthatah.
Gangé mé paarshwayorehi
Twayi gangéstu mé sthitih.*

The *Ganga Snan* festival is celebrated on the *purnima* (full moon day) of the month of *Kartika* (October/November). As the name given to the festival implies, it is a bath taken in the river Ganga which embodies purity and enlightenment. In India, to the extent it is possible, people go to the the river Ganga, otherwise they converge to some other river or the sea. In Mauritius devotees go to the sea, but many first perform the rituals at the *Ganga Talao*, at Grand Bassin before going to the sea.

Origin of the festival

The *Puranas* have accounted various reasons for the coming of Ganga to the Earth. One of the popular legends is concerned with the mythological King of Ayodha, King Sagara. It is said that King Sagara had no children. He undertook long and severe penances, at the end of which he was granted the boon of having one son from his first wife Kesini, and 60,000 sons from his second wife Sumati. The size of this family frightened Indra who felt insecure in his own kingdom.

One day King Sagara was performing the *Ashwamedha Yajna*, as a pointer to asserting himself as the supreme ruler. The sacrifice involved letting loose a horse as a challenge to anybody defying his sovereignty. He would have to fight all challengers who took possession of the horse and see that it came back to him safe. He would thus establish himself as the supreme king after subduing all his rivals. Indra felt threatened. He came down to earth and stealthily took the horse to Patala, the subterranean zone. He hid it near Sage Kapila who was sitting in deep meditation. The sixty thousand sons went in search of the horse and finally reached the spot where the sage was. Believing that the sage had stolen the horse, they woke him up from his meditation and threatened him. Angry at his being awakened from his trance, he cursed and reduced them to ashes.

Sage Narad apprised King Sagara of the fate of his sons. He immediately sent his grandson, Anshuman, to the sage to implore for forgiveness. Ansuman's humility appealed to the sage who informed him that his uncles' lives would be restored if the ashes were washed by the water of Ganga. As Ganga was in heaven she had to be propitiated and brought down to earth. King Sagara, his grandson Anshuman, and great grandson Dilipa performed *tapasya*s (austerities), but to no avail. Finally, Bhagiratha, the son of Dilipa, undertaking the most severe penances and undergoing untold sacrifices appealed to Bramha. Ganga had to give in and agreed to come to earth but needed assistance to cushion her fall. Shiva readily accepted to take her in His matted lock.

It is said that Ganga divided herself into three parts. The first part came to the earth, known as *Ganga* and led by Lord Vishnu, the next went to *Patala* (nether lands) known as *Bhagirath*, and the last one found its way to heaven as *Mandakeenee*. The water of Ganga washed away the ashes of the sons of King Sagara, and they got salvation.

Bathing in the Ganga implies purification which is not to be taken only in its physical sense but rather to the in-depth meaning of one soul's purification. By taking a bath in the *Ganga* one's sins are washed away and the heart is cleaned of the impurities heaped over the past lifetimes.

Bhisma Pitamaha

Another link is with King Santanu, in the epic *Mahabharata*. Santanu fell in love with Ganga who accepted to marry him on the promise that she would dispose of their offsprings as she wished. If Santanu for any reason tried to probe into her doings, she would instantly desert him. Santanu agreed to abide by the conditions. Of their wedlock seven children were born. Ganga took each child at his birth and killed it. When the eighth child was born, Santanu could not stay mute any longer, the bond of fatherly love inclined him to question her. She left him instantly and went away, leaving the child to him. That child was Bhisma Pitamaha, one of the most reverential figures of the *Mahabharata*.

Celebrating the festival

After the *puja* at home devotees call at the sea. They take along with them some *pitha* (dough), flowers, sacred leaves, betel nuts, camphor, sandal stick, fruits, *abir*, *kumkum sindoor,* and a coconut. Some devotees also take *khir* and *puri* as offerings. The

Giving the arag

devotees start the *puja* by invoking Mother Ganga in the sea. They spread the *pitha* (dough) on some rock in or near the sea. They present all the offerings, reciting the associated *mantras*. Burning camphor on betel leaves they offer the light to the Mother who gracefully carries it away on her breast. They then perform the *arag* (offering of water), and to close the ceremony they break the coconut. The first piece is reverentially given to Mother Ganga. Sometimes an officiating *pujari* (priest) may be present to help with the rituals and to hold discourses. He ends the ceremony with a *hawan* (fire worship) which is performed in a *hawan kund* (sacrificial pit) by offering *ahutis* (ghee and mixture of grains).

After the ceremony the devotees go for a bath in the sea with *Har har Ganga! Har har Ganga!* on the lips. Many have a bath before the rituals. Though of late it has become a practice for many devotees to break their fast soon after, yet according to many this day should be one of fasting and penance. At the time of parting in the evening the devotees feel happy and fulfilled. They express the wish to be back with their families again the year after, reminding themselves of the prayer that Mother Sita made to her -

> *"Mother, pray accomplish my desire,*
> *That I may return with my husband*
> *And his younger brother and worship you."*

Vishnupadi

Ganga is also known as *Vishnupadi*, which means that it takes its source from the foot of Vishnu. It is said that it emerged from the sweat (perspiration) of Vishnu's toes. This explanation is likely to baffle the imagination of many. But one has to consider that among Hindus reverence is paid to elders by bending low and touching their feet. And sometimes youngsters go a step further by surrendering themselves and lying prostrate at their feet. And most probably Ganga before leaving her celestial abode sought blessing from Lord Vishnu by flowing through His toes.

Guru Nanak

Guru Nanak was born on 15 April 1469 in a small town west of Lahore, Punjab, and died on 22 September 1539. His early life was spent in business and family life. In 1499 he went on mission preaching a message of salvation, and returned after twenty years. He then founded a village, Kartapur in Sialkot district (now in Pakistan) where along with some followers he gave himself to meditation, religious outlook and worldly activities.

His Message

Nanak's massage was inspired from the *Sants*, a group of mystical poets among whom was Kabir. They believed in a 'Nameless' and Formless' eternal God who manifested Himself as the Creator and Sustainer of the Universe, and lay within the human heart and soul. Nanak as many others opposed the caste system of the Hindus and the worshipping of idols, though he accepted the theory of *karma* and the transmigration of souls. To him the Omnipresent responded only to devotion and sacrifice; the individual was to detach himself from the materialistic world, attach himself to God and seek liberation. The liberation depended on God's grace, expressed through an innervoice. The need for *brahmins*, idols and external rituals did not arise. It was only by living a divine life discarding the five evils – lust, greed, anger, attachment and pride that one could reach God.

Kartapur

At Kartapur Nanak spent his time preaching, meditating and chanting *kirtans,* and soon emerged as the leader of both spiritual and public life. His contributions to the Sikh scriptures - the *Adi Granth* or the *Guru Granth Sahib* , and his influential teachings made of him the first *guru* of the Sikhs. Sikh comes from the Sanskrit word *shishya* (disciple), and refers to the ancient concept of *guru-shishya* relationship. With the Sikh faith institutionalised, the concept of *guru* too was firmly established. It moved in succession in every generation. The succession of *gurus* was seen not as one person following another, but one person following himself. Though the body was different yet it was inhabited by the same spirit, the original *guru,* and it was Guru Nanak himself in all the succeeding *gurus*. With the contribution of the successive *gurus* the *Adi Granth* gathered such high veneration that the tenth and last *guru*, Guru Gobind Singh,

The sacred texts

advocated the shifting of *guru* adoration to the worship of the *Adi Granth*. On important religious festivals, the *Adi Granth* is worshipped continuously (non-stop) for two days and two nights by devotees taking relays. The *Adi Granth* is also taken out in procession to the accompaniment of devotional songs and music. The Sikh temples, *gurudwaras,* are decorated and donations are made by every householder.

Shri Sathya Sai Baba

Shri Sathya Sai Baba is now in his second birth in the Trinity of Sai Baba incarnations. In his first birth he came as Shirdhi Sai Baba, the revered godman of the Shirdi village in Maharashtra, India. Before his death in 1918 he informed his trusted followers that he would take birth again as the second Sai. Hence the present reincarnation of his on 23rd November 1926 in Puttaparthi, a village in the Anantar district of Andhra Pradesh. As Sathya Sai Baba he will live for ninety years and will presumably leave his mortal coil in the year 2016. In his last birth in the Trinity of Baba incarnations he will be Prema Sai Baba. He has already described some of the physical and spiritual features of his next and last incarnation to many of his intimates.

In his first birth Baba came as the power of Shiva, presently he is the joint incarnation of Shiva and Shakti, and in the next birth he will be Shakti.

Baba's birth

Baba belongs to an agricultural family with deep religious moorings, fine memories and literary traditions. Born of a 'pre-chosen' parentage - Shri Venkappa Raju as father and Shrimati Eshwaramma as mother, he endeared himself to the whole family which besides the parents consisted of three sons and two daughters. He is the fourth of the five children and his childhood name is Satya Narayan Raju.

His birth was preceded by auspicious omens. Musical instruments emitted melodious sounds by themselves, and a snake appeared under his bed to welcome him. He was born with a mole on his cheek. He had himself covered with scented *vibhuti* materialised out of his tiny little hands. With his charming personality, kindness, intelligence and spiritual devotion he later endeared himself to all the village folk. At the age of fourteen he left his elder brother's house where he was staying to go to his devotees. He felt that his devotees were in dire need of him.

Baba was a good student and his pleasant manners won him the affection of all his classmates and teachers. His miracles like materialising fruits, sweets and stationery items out of his palm confirmed his divine attainment, and brought all his classmates and teachers closer to him. And this feature of creating unusual divine objects out of his hands till now has remained a striking source of wonder to all, in particular to the ever increasing number of devotees at Prasanthi Nilayan .

Baba keeps confirming himself of an *avatar*. He has given vision of himself as Shirdi Sai Baba, and many a time revealed himself as the particular deity a devotee desires of him. To convince his devotee of his *avatar* he often performs miracles. For example he manifests himself in the dream of the devotee, or, appears fleetingly before him at his call, or has *vibhuti* streaming out of pictures of deities in his house. During a *satsang* he may cause a flower to roll down from his image and fall to the ground with a tickling sound, or may sometimes allow his presence be felt by the sound of steps. Instances of having performed miracles on people suffering from incurable diseases or of helping devotees to overcome their unbearable pains and sufferings or of even bringing back corpses to life have remained to this day unique and unparalleled. About these miracles Baba says that they are meant for "planting the seed of faith in the mind of non-believers, and fostering humility and veneration towards a Higher Power". The worldly boons are only granted so that mankind can turn towards God.

Prasanthi Nilayan Ashram
Sai Baba has founded the Prasanthi Nilayan Ashram (Abode of Supreme Peace) at Prasanthi in the year 1950. The Abode is served by his devotees known as the *Seva Dal* The devotees consist of men, women, boys and girls of all communities. They have completely surrendered themselves to Baba, and their duties consist of maintaining and promoting the services of the *Ashram*. They clean utensils, maintain order and discipline at the place, and take on various other assignments. Their efficiency backed by their deep love and spirit of service make of the *Ashram* the all-perfect divine abode of bliss to all visitors.

All the year round devotees from all over the world congregate to this place of felicity as swarms of bees in quest of honey. And when once they are there they surrender themselves to Baba with unalloyed love and devotion. Baba provides each devotee with an experience unique to him. The devotee forgets everything and delves deep into the spiritual lake of love and surrender. When memory comes back to him, the mind awakes and he is imbued with the alchemy that has transformed him and everything around him into divine. He becomes a picture of light, delight and felicity. He is awakened from the slumber of ignorance. The mind and intellect do not wander anymore into the by-lanes of sensual enjoyment and material acquisition. His soul has found eternal rest. It has attained union with Baba.

However one should not conclude that only those devotees who call on him at the *Ashram* are dear to him. He is close to anybody however far he may be. All Baba wants is faith and complete surrender to God, or to any particular deity one worships. He unconditionally responds to the devotee. His aim is to bring mankind towards perfection and on the path of Godhood.

Baba gives his *darshan* (blessing) at the Prashanti Nitayan usually every morning and evening. When he comes out for *darshan* in his yellow attire of matchless splendour the devotee is expected to sit peacefully at the seat allotted and concentrate on absorbing the spiritual vibrations of bliss and elevation streaming out of him. While on his tour he takes letters from devotees who have expressed their problems and are seeking for help. Sometimes he allows the members present to do the *pad namaskar* (salutation by touching his feet). At the time of *darshan*, or at any time at Prasanthi Nilayan one has to observe strict discipline. Wearing of simple clothes (clean, sober and fairly loose), keeping of silence, avoiding taking of eatables and above all behaving in a respectable manner is strongly recommended. Sometimes Baba may himself break the silence by speaking to some devotees or even by cracking some jokes. *Kirtans* and *bhajans* are a daily feature of the *Ashram*.

One of the means through which Baba works for the betterment of mankind is by seeing and guiding those who call on him. Those who go to him may among others be -

O Sai, I seek Thy blessings

(1) devotees of God, who are already on the spiritual

path and seek enlightenment for futher progress.

(2) social workers who are in need of advice to implement their plans.

(3) statesmen and high officials who have been inspired by Baba and his teachings, and seek advice on some particular issues, or on Baba's own projects.

(4) those near and around Baba who need continued reviewing for the spreading of his teachings.

When Baba gives interviews he sometimes performs some miracles like materialising *vibhuti*, fruits, rings. As stated earlier. this is only to convince the devotees of the supernatural powers that *avatars* are endowed with. They should not give undue consideration to these miracles, nor should they brand themselves of being the only favourites of Baba. It is the *karma* of the past life that they are reaping. To be always with him, they should strive for perfection and be worthy of his teachings.

Baba has always striven for social service, education and duty, and in this regard has implemented a number of projects. The main ones are -

(1) organising of summer courses in Indian culture and spirituality at Whitefield. The first one was held in 1972

(2) setting up of the Sri Sai Institute of Higher Learning in 1982, and which now confirms itself as a leading university

(3) launching a global movement - the EHV (Education in Human Values)

(4) opening of a well-equipped hospital where highly qualified doctors provide special care.

(5) publishing of a monthly journal in 1958 - *Sanathana Sarathi (Eternal Charioteer),* the vehicle for the spreading of all his divine messages and teachings.

His message

Baba's message is one of universal love and brotherhood of man. This is seen in the sacred symbol of his Unity of Religions which bears a cross, fire, wheel, crescent moon and star, and the *Aum*. The cross stands for the elimination of the ego I, the fire for the destruciton of the lower instincts of man, the wheel symbolises the wheel of righteousness, the crescent moon and the star for the unfailing faith and devotion to Good and God, and finally the *Aum* for spiritual inspiration and success.

Most of the teachings of Baba originate from the sacred scriptures like the *Vedas*, *Upanishads, Puranas, Gita,* and *Bible,* and they are supported through instances from the lives of the great heroes as Rama, Krishna, Christ, Mohammed, Buddha, Zoroastra, Ramakrishna, and Tagore. He himself advocates " I have not come to set afoot a new cult ", his mission he says is "to reconstruct the ancient highway to spirituality, to revive the *Vedas* and the Scriptures". He emphasises on the existence of "One God" - the theory of monotheism of the Hindu cult. And along with supreme devotion and chanting of God's name (*namasmaran*) to attain *moksha* (liberation), he preaches *sattya* (truth), *dharma* (righteousness), *shanti* (peace), *prema* (love) and service to man.

Gita Jayanti

The *Bhagavad Gita* is part of the great epic *Mahabharata* which deals with the conflict between good and evil. Good is represented by the five Pandavas supported by Krishna and the wicked are the Kauravas who number a hundred brothers.

Gita Jayanti (birthday of the *Bhagavad Gita*) is held on the *ekadashi* (eleventh day) of the bright fortnight (*suklapaksh*) of the month of *Margasirsa* (December/January). On this day Sanjaya started delivering the running commentary of the battle between the Pandavas and the Kauravas at Kurukshetra to King Dhristarastra. The king was blind, not only physically but spiritually as he unhesitatingly supported the unrighteous claim of his son, Duryodhana to the throne. He therefore appealed to Sanjaya to acquaint him with all the events taking place on the battlefield.

This *Gita* (Song of the Blessed Lord) has come straight from the mouth (*moukhvrind*) of the Lord. The two armies, Pandavas and Kauravas, ready to fight each other had gathered on the Kurukshetra battlefield. The conch was blown, the signal given and the war was about to begin. The great archer, Arjuna of the Pandavas brothers requested his charioteer Krishna, the Lord Himself, to drive him in the middle of the field where the two armies were facing each other. He glanced and saw but members of his own family, close relatives and friends on both sides. He became despondent and gave up his weapon. It was then and in that dramatic setting that the Lord gave His message, the *Gita* which has come to stay for eternity. Through Arjuna, the message was meant to the whole of mankind. It contains the very quintessence of the *Vedas*, the very knowledge one needs to attain *moksha*.

Background

The Pandavas and the Kauravas were closely related being the sons of two brothers. The Pandavas were the rightful heir to the throne. Duryodhana, heading the Kauravas, was jealous and coveting the crown challenged Yudhisthir, the eldest brother of the Pandavas and the rightful heir to the throne, to a crooked game of dice. Yudhistir lost the game. He was forced to go on exile along with his brothers and their common consort, Draupadi for twelve years, followed by an additional year during which they would have to live *incognito*. If they happened to be recognised, the banishment period would start anew. But if they returned after fulfilling all the conditions they would be given their due.

When the Pandavas came back on completion of their exile, they sent their cousin and friend Krishna to the Kauravas to claim their due. Duryodhana, the leader of the Kauravas, flatly refused. When Krishna came with the Kauravas' refusal, war became inevitable. Both the Kauravas and the Pandavas sought the help of Krishna and called on Him. Krishna offered to help both and gave them the choice between having Him and His army. He also informed them that He would not fight in the war. The Kauravas chose the army, while Pandavas unhesitatingly took the Lord who became the charioteer of Arjuna.

At the beginning of the war it is worth noting the attitude of the leaders of both armies. Duryodhana, proud and overconfident, started by immediately giving orders to all, even to his elders - the great grand-father Bhisma, and his *guru* Drona. On the other side Arjuna seeing the close relatives in the two armies got bewildered and took the decision of not waging the war. But as a good disciple he sought advice before taking a decision, and he appealed to Krishna -

Karpanya dushopahata svabhavah prichani twaam dharmasammudhah chetah yat sreyasyam nischitam bruhitan me sishyasteham shodhi mam twam prapannam."

"My heart is overpowerd by the taint of pity;
My mind is confused as to duty .I ask thee..
Tell me decisively what is good for me. I am thy disciple.
Instruct me who has taken refuge in thee."

It was then that flowed the glorious message of the Lord; the hidden truth was revealed.

Message

In this world there is ceaseless conflict between good and evil. Though both are inherent in the creation, yet man is aware that evil is not divine. It has to be avoided. Man should try to be good and divine, and the purpose of life is to go even beyond that good and to merge in the Ultimate Good, the Lord. However this struggle to a divine and spiritual life may seem to collapse faced with the ruthless and lawless forces. Krishna recommends never to give up the struggle as He promises to come to the rescue when the forces of adversity become unbearable

"For the protection of the good, for the destruction of the wicked and for the establishment of righteouness: I am born in every age."

Paritarnaya sadhoonaam vinaas sya cha dushkritam Dharmasansthapanaarthaya sambhavaami yuge yuge.

Krishna advocates that man has to know himself and see through the forces that pin him down to ignorance. To this end He has endowed every human being with knowledge and wisdom. Man has to rise above the world of duality and the pairs of opposites - success and failure, honour and dishonour, birth and death. He has to attain eternal bliss and immortality, and His gospel is one of action, it teaches the performance of one's duty in society, the life of active struggle but without allowing one's inner being to be affected by outer surroundings. Above all He insists that all actions be offered to God without expecting the fruit of those actions.

"Thy right is to work only, but never to its fruits. Let not the fruit of action be thy motive, nor let thy attachment be to inaction."

Karmany eva dhikaras te ma phalesu kadacana Ma karmaphalahetur bhur ma te sango 'stv akarmani.

The stable value should be remembrance of God, all the rest being added to life as adjuncts. The attitude of the mind should be ever tuned to Him so that it is released for ever from the clutches of *Maya*. How to attach oneself to the Lord ! This is done by living in the spirit of His teachings which should not be taken as a theoretical exercise but implemented in practical life. The theory without being put into practice will result into the one being blind and the other being lame. The blind needs the eyes of the lame to look forward, and the lame needs the legs of the blind to move forward. There should be the synthesis of knowledge and action.

Krishna impels man to go beyond the *gunas* of nature - the *tamasic* (state of ignorance), *rajasic* (the state of passion) and the *satvic* (the state of knowledge). These *gunas* are all the time inherent in man and manifest themselves as the mind direct them. The *tamasic* is the lower stage of behaviour, the *rajasic*- the middle stage and the *satvic* the higher stage. This could be explained through the analogy of fire. Fire has the three attributes - smoke, which is *tamasic* and is unpleasant and harmful; heat which is *rajasic* and can be both pleasant and unpleasant; and light which is *satvic* and is pleasant and desirable. Man should have complete control of the mind and be free from desire as the forces of destruction like lust, greed and anger arise out of it.

Once above the three *gunas* man should attempt to reach the Supreme Being. Krishna has advocated three paths to this end - *Karma Yoga* (Action), *Jnaya Yoga* (Knowledge) and the *Bhakti Yoga* (Devotion). The *yogi,* the knowledgeable who reaches the trancendental state and sees God everywhere and in everything attains his goal through the *Jnaya Yoga*. The man devoted to action with a controlled mind and in a spirit of *tyaag* takes the *Karma Yoga*. And finally the one who surrenders himself to the Lord through prayers, meditation and to His service reaches Him through the *Bhakti Yoga*. To the common man *Bhakti Yoga* seems to be the easiest path and the assurance has already been given -

Man mana bhava mad-bhakto mad-yajee nam-namaskurn Mamavaishyosi satyam ta platigora priyasimay.

"Fix thy mind on me, be devoted to me, sacrifice to me, bow down to me, Thou shalll come to me, truly do I promise unto thee for thou art dear to me ."

Bibliography

Bandyopadhyay Pranab - *Hindu Faith and Religion*, Image India, Calcutta, India, 1987.

Beswick Ethel - *The Hindu Gods*, Crest Publishing House, New Delhi, India, 1993.

Gupta M. Shakti - *Festivals, Fairs and Fasts of India,* Clarion Books, New Delhi, India, 1990.

Kumar Shedev - *The Vision of Kabir: Love poems of a 15th Century Weaver Sage*, Motilal Banarasidas Indological Publishers, Delhi, India, 1984.

Mitchel A.B. - *Hindu Gods and Goddesses,* UBS Publishers Distributors Ltd., New Delhi, India, 1993.

Ramdoyal Ramesh - *Festivals of Mauritius*, Editions de l'Océan Indien Ltée, Mauritius, 1990.

Ruhela S.P. - *Sri Sathya Sai Baba - His Life and Divine Role*, Vikas Publishing House Pvt. Ltd., New Delhi, India, 1993.

Sharma B.N. - *Festivals of India*, Abhinav Publications, New Delhi, India, 1978.

Swami Harshanand - *Hindu Gods and Goddesses*, Shri Ramakrishna Math, Madras, India, 1981.

Swami Sivananda - *Hindu Fasts and Festivals*, The Divine Life Society, Shivanandanagar, Uttar Pradesh, India, 1993.

Swami Venkatesananda - *Freedom from Sorrow,* Divine Life Society, Madras, India, 1961.

Encyclopedia of Religion - Macmillan Publishing Company, New York, USA, 1987.

Glossary

Aarti - Ceremony of waving a lighted lamp or camphor round an idol
Abhishek - Consecration
Abir - Shocking pink powder
Agni - Fire, God of fire
Ahuti - Offerings used in fire-worship as ghee and grains
Akash - Ether, sky, heaven
Akshat - Rice grains
Amrit - Ambrosia, nectar of immortality
Amritakalasha - Pot of ambrosia
Anjouli/Anjouri - Handful
Ans/Ansh - Part, essence
Arag/Argyam - Libation in honour of a deity
Artha - Wealth
Ashram - Abode for religious and social activities, charitable institution
Asura - Demon
Atchman/Atchmanam - Rinsing of mouth with water before religious ceremony, sipping of water
Avahan - Invocation
Avatar - Divine birth, incarnation
Amla/Awala - *fruit de cythere* (Fch), *Phyllanthus embelico*

Baitka - Meeting place for social and religious activities
Bajra - millet, cereal, *Pennistum typhoides*
Bansh - Lineage
Bar - Banyan tree
Barfi - Indian sweet made of milk
Bhajan - Devotional song
Bhakti - Devotion
Bhang - Intoxicating drink
Bidaye - Send-off
Bilva/Bilwa - Bael tree, *Aegle marmelos*

Brahmin - the priestly caste
Bringa - Bee

Chandan - Sandal tree
Chandrama - Moon
Channa - Chickpeas
Chiendent - Conchgrass (*durva/dharba*)
Chirchirya (bhojpuri) - Holy grass used in religious ceremonies
Chutney - Pungent Indian condiment, sauce

Daan - Gift, donation
Daani - Donor
Dakshina - Gift usually to a Brahmin or guru
Darshan - Sight, view, appearance
Deva/Devta - God, usually a minor god
Devi - Goddess, female aspect of Shiva
Dhaan - Unhusked paddy
Dharba/Durva - Sacrificial grass used in worship (*kush*), *Poa Cynasuroides*
Dharma - Righteousness, duty, discipline
Dholak - Drum, musical instrument
Dhup/Dhupam - Burnt perfume, incense
Dip/Dipak/Dipam - Lamp
Duta - Messenger

Gandha/Gandham - Perfume
Gandharva - Celestial being
Ganga jal - Water from the river Ganges
Gehun - Wheat flour
Ghar - House
Ghat - Bathing place on a riverside
Gopi - Cowherd girl
Graha - Satellite, Maleficient spirit

Gramya - Pertaining to a village
Gulal - Coloured powder
Gular - Holy fig tree whose flowers and stems are usedin in worship
Guna - Attribute, quality.
Guru - Teacher, preceptor
Gurudwar - Sikh place of worship

Haldi - Turmeric, saffron
Hawan - Fire worship
Hawan kund - Sacrificial pit for fire worship

Istadeva/Istadevta - Chosen deity
Indra - God of Rain, God of Heaven

Jal - Water
Janeo - Sacred thread usually worn by a brahmin
Japmala - Rosary of beads
Jawain - Carrom seed, sorghum
Jeera - Cuminseed, aromatic flavouring seed
Jhal - Cymbal

Kaajal - Collyrium prepared from soot
Kala - Supernatural power (Lord Krishna born with 16 *kalas*)
Kalash - Pitcher, symbol of divine power
Kalash Sthapna - Consecration of *kalash*
Kama - Pleasures of life
Kanwar - Frame made of *ravenal* (Travellers' tree) or bamboo stems and decorated with coloured cloth and paper, pictures, bells, etc., carried by a pilgrim
Karwa - Earthen pot with sprout
Katha - Discourse
Katori - Small bowl or cup

Kavi - Poet
Ketaki - Flower, *Pandanus Odoratissimum*
Khir - Sweetmeal made of rice, milk and sugar
Kirtan - Hymn singing
Kitchri - Savoury meal of rice, lentils and other ingredients
Koncha - Knot at one end of a *sari* containing consecrated offerings
Kool - Lineage, same line of descent
Kumkum - Red powder used in worship
Kush - similar to the *vetiver*, used in worship as the *durva*, *Poa Cynosuroides*

Ladoo - Indian sweets usually made of gram flour
Laurier - (*Tej patta*), Baytree *Laurus Nobilis, Oleander* tree
Lawa - Roasted *dhaan* or maize, parched rice
Linga/Lingum - Phallic symbol of Shiva
Lithi - Thick cake made with unleavened flour usually on an open fire
Lota - Pot

Madar - Swallow wort plant, *Calotropis gigantia*
Makhan - Butter
Madhyaratri - Midnight
Mandir - Temple
Manshik Shristi - Born of mind
Mantra - Hymn, incantation
Mattu - Cattle
Maula - Lord, Leader, Preacher
Maya - Illusion, in particular the natural world regarded as unreal
Mela - Fair, big gathering
Methunik Shristi - Taking birth from the body
Mewa samosha - Indian sweet made of flour and stuffed with a preparation of milk and sugar

Modak - Indian sweet rice balls sweetmeat
Moksha - Liberation, beatitude
Moong - Green lentils (as kidney beans)
Moukhvrind - Given by word of mouth
Muhurtta - Auspicious time
Muni - Saint, holy man

Naivedya - Fruits offered to a deity
Nakshatra - Planet, asterism
Namaskar - Salute
Nazar - Evil eye
Neem - Holy tree, margosa tree, *Azadirachta Melia*
Nirjal - Abstaining from taking even water while fasting

Paan ke bira - spiced betel leaf stuffed with ground areca, lime, etc., usually taken after a meal or on auspicious occasions
Padma - Lotus
Padya/padyam - Foot
Panchagavya - Five sacred items produced by the cow, usually milk, curd, butter, urine, dung or ghee
Panchamrit - Mixture of five ingredients offered to a deity
Panchang - Hindu almanach
Pandit - Learned brahmin, Hindu officiating priest
Pankar - Holy tree whose leaves and stems are used in worship
Parikrama - Circumambulation
Patala - Netherworld
Peepul/pipul - Holy fig tree, sacred bodhi tree, *Ficus religiosa*
Pindam/pindaan - Oblation to the manes
Pichkari - syringe
Pitha - Dough
Pongal - Boiled
Pooah - Sweet cake made from a mixture of flour, milk and sugar
Poungipal - Betel nuts
Pradakshina - Circumambulation

Prakrivit - Uncultivated, raw
Prasad - Offerings to a deity, consecrated food
Prathna - Prayer
Prema - Love
Prithvi - Earth
Puja - Religious ceremony
Puja ghar - Prayer room
Pujari - Officiating priest
Purana - Hindu sacred text
Purushartas - Goals of human life
Purnahuti - Cclosing ceremony
Puri - Dough rolled flat and fried in ghee or clarified butter
Pushp/Pushpam - Flower
Putra - Son

Rakhi - Silk thread, silken amulet
Rangoli - floor decoration made with rice powder on auspicious occasions
Rasi - Zodiac sign
Rishi - Holy man, a saint
Rot - Sweet cake made of flour, milk and ghee

Saligram - Oval stone representing Lord Vishnu
Samadhi - meditation
Samsara - Cycle of birth and death
Sandhya - Ceremonious lighting of lamp before dusk
Sankalp - Taking a vow
Sankha - Conch
Saptadana - Seven grains
Sari - Garment worn by Hindu women
Sarson - Mustard plant, *Brassica Compostris*
Sati - Chaste woman
Satsang - Meeting for discourse, prayers and chanting of hymns
Sattya - Truth
Shakti - Energy, Shiva's energy through His consort Parvati
Shanti - Peace
Shastra - Weapon
Shishya - Disciple, pupil

Shivala - Temple
Shradda - Oblation
Sindour - Vermillion
Sindrawata - Dainty container of vermillion
Snan/Snanam - Bath
Soma - Moon
Soudh - Clean, unpolluted
Soupari - Betel nuts, areca nuts
Surya - Sun
Swami - Learned Holy man
Swayamvar - Princely gathering where a princess chooses her own bridegroom

Tambul - Betel leaf
Tapasya - Austerity
Tarpan - Oblation
Thali - Metal plate
Til - Sesame seeds, gingelly seeds, *Sesamum Indicum*
Tilak - Sacred mark applied on the forehead
Tithi - Lunar day, date
Tulsi - Holy basil leaf, *Ocimum Sanctum*

Upanishad - Hindu sacred text
Urad - Lentils, black *moong*, *Phaseolus radiatus*

Vara - Boon
Vasant - Spring
Vastra/Vastram - Cloth
Vata - Banyan tree
Vayu - Wind, God of Wind
Ved - Doctor
Veda - Hindu sacred text
Veena - Lute
Vetiver/Vetivert - Whort flowered bent grass, cushion grass, *Vetivaria*, similar to *kush*
Vibhuti - Ashes, usually from fire worship
Visarjan - Closing, departure
Vrat - Fast

Yajna - Sacrifice, ceremony
Yam - Guardian of Hell
Yoni - Female organ of generation

Editions Capucines
20 Avenue des Capucines
Quatre Bornes
Mauritius
Tel/Fax (230) 464 1563